Cat
Names

THE BEST EVER BOOK OF
CAT NAMES

Eleanora Walker

Illustrations by Alan Daniel

GALAHAD BOOKS
New York

Previously published as CAT NAMES: THE BEST BOOK EVER Text copyright © 1984 by Eleanora Walker. Illustrations © 1984 by Alan Daniel.

First Galahad Books edition published in 1995.

Galahad Books
A division of Budget Book Service, Inc.
386 Park Avenue South
New York, NY 10016

Galahad Books is a registered trademark of Budget Book Service, Inc.

Published by arrangement with HarperCollins Publishers.

Library of Congress Catalog Card Number: 95-75036

ISBN: 0-88365-892-5

Printed in the United States of America.

For
Walter Tevis

Acknowledgments

I would like to thank the following people for their contributions to this book:

ALASKA
Liz Hampton

ARIZONA
Rosabelle Furcap, Sara and Marv Jacobs, Amy Macnamara

CALIFORNIA
Herb Gold, Fritz Leiber

COLORADO
Barbara and Bill Stroud

CONNECTICUT
Juno Gendron, Anne Gorman, Roberta and John Hamilton, Joanne Woodward and Paul Newman

FLORIDA
Babs Brownlie, Betty and Toby Bruce, Love Dean, Lawrence Holmes, Margaret Macdonald

HAWAII
Allen Stamper

IOWA
Arabella and Sid Tubbs

KANSAS
John Collier

KENTUCKY

Tom Blues, Margaret Buranen, Betty and Andy Eckdahl, Will Iovenko, Overton Chenault Kavanaugh, Elmer Maggard, Gurney Norman, Amy and Sarah Petit, Ellie and Peter Welt, Sonny Wigginton, Sue and Gus Wiley, Nancy Yearsley

NEW JERSEY

Diana Jessop

NEW MEXICO

Christine and Davis Mather, Harris Richard

NEW YORK

Ray Alongi, Christine Amsler, Larry Ashmead, Domenico Augello, Joan Avril, Priscilla and Alan Brandt, Elizabeth Cater, John Coe, Cynthia Collins, Dominique De Anfrasio, Ruth and Ken Deardoff, C. Linda Dingler, Meg Eisenberg, Loring Eutemey, Anne Freedgood, Molly Friedrich, Frank Gioli, Nancy Hall, Heather Hamilton, Michaela Hamilton, Douglas and Michael Heller, Gertrude Huston, Beena Kamlani, Marcia Kaufman, Trevor Kaufman, Hilary Knight, Katharine Kreilkamp, Jill Lesser, Stuart Morden, Jim Mueller, Craig Nelson, Rosemary O'Connell, Betty Prashker, Hal Reiter, Robert Rye, Dr. Charles Schaubhut, Sioux Schueller, Roz and Stan Smith, Herry Teltscher, Walter Tevis, Bill Van Assen, Jason Walker, Margaret Wimberger, Ann Worthin, Amy Zachary, Jean Ziefel

OHIO

Julie McGory, Will Tevis

PENNSYLVANIA

Ponder Goembel

TEXAS

Shirley Pope, Sal Stallone

VIRGINIA

James Tiptree, Jr.

My heartfelt thanks go to Eleanor Goudreau and Bob Russell, who programmed and ran *Operation Catnip*, which alphabetized over 4000 cat names. Without their help this author's mind might have cracked.

Contents

Cat
Names

Why Write This Book?

At one point in my life I believe I fell under an enchantment. In its severest form the spell lasted for seven years, which is the reason I know it was an enchantment in the first place, and during this time I was committed to feeding and caring for many homeless cats in the alleys and on waterfronts of New York. I fed them and named them and they multiplied, so I took in many litters of kittens, whom I bathed and de-fleaed and tamed and named to increase their prospects of adoption. There were so many kittens I long ago lost count, yet none of them went out into the world nameless and the naming of them was not a difficult matter. My first caught were Humphrey, Dolly and Bean Blossom, who became my own personal cats. Then there were Mary-Margaret, Tiffany, Beau, Boris, Pandora and Polly Flinders. The exquisite Abigail found crying at the foot of a garbage can. Coffin and Diana, Bubble and Squeak, Andrew and Simon. Fitzwillie, Fitzpatrick, Fitzgerald and Fitzsimmon (and now Fitzcaraldo). Snapdragon, Crosspatch, Barnacle and George. Piecrust, Beeswax and Driftwood. Cobweb and Moonbeam. Jasmine. Sweet Molly Malone. These are just a few who passed through the portals of the Adieu Tristesse Foundling Home for Cats. Much to my chagrin those carefully chosen names were usually tossed out the window and the kittens rebaptized by their new owners.

1

I learned to bite my tongue, and I took it for granted that naming a cat came easily to most people. Indeed, most people can come up with a name though some spend a lifetime apologizing for it. However, there are people in this world, in other respects intelligent and well-educated, who draw a blank when it comes to naming a cat. The following story is true, but the names have been changed to protect the innocent.

A mature couple acquired a mature cat from a friend who had to leave the country. The cat, an overblown beauty, had been named Gloria by her departing owner, a perfectly suitable name with which cat and master had lived happily for several years. However, "Gloria" did not sit well with the new owners since it was also the name of an old flame of the husband in question, so they set about renaming her with alacrity. They had been advised to find a name close in sound to the old one, but all they could think of was "Pretoria" and "Andrea Doria," neither of which they cared for. Noticing that she ate in a dainty way they soon hit upon Nibbles, and Nibbles she remained for about a week, after which they began to feel uneasy about their choice. It lacked sophistication and did not fit the cat's personality. Admittedly they were having difficulty in grasping her personality, which seemed to change from day to day. So they tried another name, and then another, and the children of their previous marriages pitched in, as did their occasional butler. In their haste to make her a member of the family they have bestowed a bewildering succession of names upon the poor cat in short order, none of which has turned out to be appropriate. The result is that they are royally frustrated, the cat turns a deaf ear when she is called and everyone downs another martini, butler, children and all.

Now, I am not one to go knocking on Park Avenue doors with unsolicited advice on naming cats. But it seems clear that Gloria was going through a period of adjustment in separating from one master, whose habits and rhythm of life she had grown accustomed to, and settling into a household with quite different sounds and smells and comings and goings. In short she was suffering from a temporarily fragmented personality. Hence the difficulty. The proper approach for this couple would have been to bide their time until Gloria had settled in and was relaxed and comfortable, meanwhile using some noncommital term of endearment such as puss, kitty, kumquat or dumpling. Different conditions and people bring out different facets of a cat's personality. The Gloria who lived with a bachelor in a quiet brownstone may well be a very different cat from the one who settles into a large, bright apartment with a lot of social activity. Only time will tell. And when time has told will be the time to name her.

Neither wealth, charm, intelligence nor social position came to the aid of this family in this predicament. And they are not alone. Many a harried mother has to contend with a brood of squabbling children trying to name a kitten. No one comes up with a name that is so clearly perfect that everyone will accept it. Mother tries to get in her two cents' worth, knowing full well that she will be responsible for the creature's upbringing, but no one is buying her choice either. Often she is reduced to making small lists of inoffensive names and drawing straws. No one is completely satisfied with the result, and everyone is slightly grudging and grumpy.

To top it all, I recently met a woman at a dinner party in one of these SoHo lofts that boggles the mind with its splendor, who has owned a cat for fourteen years and still hasn't thought of a name for it.

It is for such that I write this book.

Does a Cat Really Know Its Name?

I believe it does. Whether or not your cat responds to its name on a given day is a different matter. He may be miffed at the repetitive dullness of his diet, or he may have something more interesting on his mind, so he may just choose to ignore you. But I'm convinced that the more intimate the bond between you and your cat the more certain it is he knows his name, even in a household with several cats.

My first cats—Humphrey and Dolly and Bean Blossom—and I lived in a pleasant apartment in a shabby old brownstone. We who live in little buildings in New York are likely to be hemmed in by larger ones, and we learn to anticipate the appearance of the sun in various rooms at different times of the day and to follow it on its rounds. On one particular afternoon, Dolly and Bean Blossom lay entwined in their 1:30 patch of sunshine on the study floor at the front of the apartment, facing south, and Humphrey lay asleep on the captain's chair by the window, one paw over his eyes. Humphrey was a gentle, solid, affectionate cat, and I was much given to hugging and kissing him. He, in turn, was much given to climbing on my lap, where I would cradle him like a baby as I watched television of an evening, and often his gray paw would tap my cheek with gentle insistence, requesting me to gaze into his eyes rather than into the screen. As I passed him that afternoon, I contented myself with stroking his whiskers and caressing his tummy, so as not to disturb his sleep; Humphrey removed his paw, opened his eyes a slit, stretched, yawned and resumed his slumber.

Walking the length of the apartment to the bedroom, some seventy-five feet away, I encountered a large water bug about the size of the palm of my hand. Now, at that time of my life I was even less spiritually advanced than I am at present, and I screamed in horror at the sight of the lowly creature and shouted, *"Humphrey, save me!"* No sooner had I called out the words than I heard a thud followed by a thunder of cat paws galloping across the wooden floors and down the uncarpeted hallway. Within seconds Humphrey screeched to a halt on the bedroom floor, rubbing the sleep from his eyes and looking at me like a perplexed but ready Sir Galahad. I wrung my hands and pointed to the water bug, and, with a quick grasp of his duty, Humphrey pounced on it and kept it firmly underpaw till my husband arrived to dispose of it. Throughout it all, Dolly and Bean Blossom did not bestir themselves, knowing full well that they had not been called upon to deliver me, and that in good conscience they could continue to snooze in the sunshine.

Your Cat Won't Mind
What You Call It

Naming a cat is different from naming a baby and a lot more fun. The choice of a baby's name is often dictated by family, ethnic and social considerations. But in naming your cat you'll find that you are now unhampered by such. You should choose a name that is sexually appropriate because it will be less confusing to *you* if the cat that bounds home to your call of "Emily" resembles no one so much as Sylvester Stallone and is the terror of the neighborhood. This apart, you are free to be as prosaic as you please or as fanciful. You can name your cat Sam or Joe or Blue or Red or Max or Harry or Joan. Or Clytemnestra, Scheherazade, Persimmon, Pomegranate, Juniper, Joralemon or Thomas Aquinas.

Of one thing you can be sure: your cat will never turn around in later life and reproach you for its name. It makes no difference to your cat what she is called, as long as she is called it consistently.

I know a cat whose name is You Damn Fool Cat, a name bestowed in affection by the crotchety, bearded actor with whom she lives. With catlike lack of scruple, he maintains, she took advantage of his inebriated condition at a friend's party and sweet-purred him into taking her home, where, on the basis of a very conditional entrée, she has established a sixteen-year rule over his apartment and much of his life.

7

They live amicably together in a long, dim apartment in the vicinity of Gramercy Park, and in summertime he likes to take her sailing in Long Island Sound to get fresh air and sunshine. An occasional lady in a passing boat will call out excitedly, "What a sweet, pretty cat! Whatever is its name?" and the actor calls back gruffly, "You Damn Fool Cat!" "Oh, no!", cries the lady, "I mean its *name*." "You Damn Fool *Cat!*" he hollers and the lady sails on, looking perplexed and some-what abused.

It's clear the curmudgeon enjoys these exchanges and You Damn Fool Cat, sunning on the deck, is serenely indifferent to her name. Like any self-respecting cat, all she is really interested in on the plane of human-cat relations is two square meals a day, a soft pillow to sleep on and a fair amount of companionship and love.

Aptness Is All

Pause before you name. It's amazing the number of people who apologize for their cat's name.

"Oh, what a lovely cat! What's her name?"

"Lovey."

"How'd you come to call her Lovey?"

"She was a very loving kitten, and it was all I could think of." Shrug.

Lovey has a mass of long, thick, strawberry blond hair and large orange eyes, and all in all looks like Brigitte Bardot sunning herself in the garden. She is still a loving cat, but her people are probably more tuned in to other aspects of her personality. They are dimly aware that they are missing out on one of life's greater satisfactions: a truly aptly named pet, be it cat, dog, bird, rabbit or whatever. The smugness of a human who has come up with the right name for a pet has few rivals.

The aptness or felicitousness of a name often depends on sight, or sound, or circumstance.

※⁂⁂

Huntley and Brinkley, two gray pin-stripe cats, are introduced to each and every guest at the cocktail parties thrown in their Connecticut home. They belong to the sort of family in which the children are sent to Princeton and Wellesley

11

and everyone is informed on the issues of the day, including, as you might suspect, the cats.

※※ⓒ※※

A Jesuit priest of my acquaintance, after many years of service in the church, developed serious doubts about his calling. He left the priesthood and went to France where he lived for many years with a charming French noblewoman in a small château, during which time he got a cat and called it Doubting Thomas.

※※ⓒ※※

There's a small hotel of ill-repute in midtown Manhattan; on its ground floor is a pharmacy whose shelves are strangely bare of the usual items you'd expect to find there. There is, however, a wide variety of prophylactics and two resident cats, one of whom is called Rameses, the other Trojan.

※※ⓒ※※

Ambrose and Cecilia were all the rage among my friends because of the mellifluousness of their names and the poetry of their appearance. They were two white Persian cats found wandering in the sea of rubble that surrounded my midtown brownstone apartment, which, at that time, was waiting to be demolished like the rest of the block. We who live in little buildings in New York. often move from pillar to post, dictated to by the vagaries of the real-estate market. The cats were clean, which proved they weren't long lost, but so thin and ill-nourished beneath their plumes, I made no attempt to find out who lost them. Au contraire. I fattened them up and brushed their long hair till it shone like silk. They were the last word in elegance and when they walked across a room together, which they did frequently, tails fanned high over their backs, calculating the effect upon their audience, they looked like glorious sailing ships. My then husband, who rarely got the chance to name a cat (which might explain a thing or two), insisted on calling the male after the Ambrose Light Ship, which had been recently in the news.

It was a good choice. Ambrose was a big, handsome, un-ruffled cat who gazed at the world through yellow eyes. He was quietly protective of the smaller female, whom we took to be his consort. She too had a pleasant, even disposition, accepting Ambrose's attentions as quietly as he paid them, as though they were her due. They were like an amiable couple who have had money in the bank so long that nothing in life can faze them. I named her Cecilia after a new friend with whom I was greatly impressed because she was said to have had a love affair with Marlon Brando when *he* was nineteen. (Can you *imagine* such fortune in life?) Ambrose and Cecilia were adopted by the wife of a prosperous farmer from up-state New York, who cosseted them all their days and issued bulletins on their progress through life for their many admirers.

※〰️(ᴗᴗ)〰️※

Miss Pudding is the most stolid cat I have ever met. You can talk to her till you're blue in the face, heap endearments on her head and all you'll get in return is the cold shoulder. Like the suet puddings of my British childhood, the heavi-ness of her personality is apparent at first glance. Her appli-cation to be included in Terry DeRoy Gruber's book *Work-ing Cats* was rejected out of hand, her photo returned forthwith. Despite this, Miss Pudding is loved. In the bosom of her family, Miss Pudding is cherished. Many years ago she walked into a warehouse in lower Manhattan, young, starv-ing and pregnant. She was fed and sheltered by the family who owned the building, and her kittens were adopted into good homes. To repay this kindness she cleared the ware-house of rats with a speed and ferocity that were awe in-spiring. Esteemed by all, she lived and worked there till she was elderly and one of her offspring took over her job.

The children of the family moved out into the world and took Miss Pudding with them to the far different ambience of upper Madison Avenue, where they sell contemporary art glass in a small, elegant shop. Along one side of this shop runs a raised, open platform on which stand slender pedestals that hold delicate hand-blown glass objects with price tags of twenty thousand dollars. Among them Miss Pudding wanders freely where she wills, day or night, and no one turns a hair. Most remarkable of all, Miss Pudding is trusted.

※ᔔᑕᦿᕐ※

Years of gratification can be obtained from a judicious choice of name and, with a little thought, you can aptly name your pet. However, one thing is very important: be sure you want to keep your pet before naming it too aptly, because you may name it so aptly you're stuck with it willy-nilly.

Several years ago some friends of mine went to live on one of the more remote Hawaiian islands. They were restless young people who disliked convention and they lived together in the woods with a group of like-minded friends, a bit further from civilization than Walden Pond from Concord. They built wooden shacks under the trees, cooked in ovens made from oil drums and caught fish to eat and the boldest and most beautiful one among them risked his life in the surf catching the rare opihi to sell in town. Though they disliked killing animals, they were occasionally obliged to hunt for game to supplement their diet. Once when they were out in the woods they came across a young wild pig that had been badly mauled by dogs, but still had some life in him. They took him back to camp where they built their evening fire and buttered up the piglet. Then they cradled him in their arms and sang him lullabies and nursed him back to health and called him Francis Bacon.

Time passed and Francis Bacon grew larger. But in his heart he still thought of himself as a piglet whose wounds were soothed by butter and kindness, and in the evenings he would still squeeze himself onto an available lap and squeal until they sang him to sleep with lullabies. Francis got bigger and their laps got smaller and they tired of singing him lullabies, but you can't just shoo a pig so aptly named back into the wild woods. So they were stuck with him. And there they are to this day, a group of aging flower children living on a remote Hawaiian island with an aging pig who still insists upon lullabies at bedtime.

And don't think it couldn't happen with a cat.

The Process

In *Breakfast at Tiffany's,* Holly Golightly has a cat whom she willfully insists on calling Cat. This is not a good thing. It's as bad as calling a male child Boy or a female child Girl. Every cat, like every person, is unique and deserves its own name.

There are many ways to go about naming it. If you are visually inclined you can base your cat's name on some obvious physical characteristic such as size, shape, color, markings or a particular way of walking. Some people are very basic about the matter. Two cats who live in the heart of Brooklyn are called Big and Little, which is just what they are. And on Manhattan's Upper West Side two Abyssinian cats lived with a pretty girl who couldn't tell them apart except by weight; so she named one cat Light and the other Heavy. Her lover, a handsome young Frenchman, also had two cats, whom he called Dream and Star. As you might surmise, their relationship was not destined to last, her with her feet on the ground, him in the air.

If color is your field . . .

Black cats can be named:

Blackie	Ebony
Inky	Jet
Sooty	Midnight

Tarbaby	Umbra
Mandingo	Coal Dust
Othello	Anthracite

At the age of ten, one of my friends was cycling past a blackberry bush when she heard a faint miaow from the middle of it. Dismounting, she found a small black kitten, which she took home and christened Blackberry.

White cats can be called:

Whitey	Vanilla
Snowy	Whitewash
Snowhite	White Cloud
Snowflake	Blanche
Snowball	Bianca
Snowdrop	Daisy
Snowflower	Ivory
Snowfire	Rinso
Snowman	Soapsuds
Ermine	Marble
Eggshell	Crystal
Eggwhite	Jack Frost
Eggcream	Oyster

That same friend, cycling past the same blackberry bush the next day, heard another faint miaow and discovered a small white kitten, which she took home and christened Whiteberry.

Red, yellow, orange cats run to:

Red	Amarillo
Ginger	Honey
Pumpkin	Cinnamon
Peaches	Paprika
Turnip	Sunshine
Mustard	Sunburst
Custard	Gingerbread
Marmalade	Carmel
Citrus	Goldfarb
O.J.	Amber
Pizza	Ochre
Pekoe	Sienna
Saffron	

17

That same young lady on the bicycle grew up to be a menace to pedestrians, got an orange cat and called it Gingersnaps.

Brown cats can be called:

Nutmeg	Sorrel
Toast	Kahlua
Cocoa	Mahogany
Mocha	Tobacco
Umber	Nicotine

Blue cats and gray cats are called:

Blue	Smoky
Bluebell	Shadow
Bluebird	Gray
Bluebottle	Ashes
Ironblue	Haze
Indigo	Charcoal

Lucy Blueberry summers on the island of Nantucket. Ash Wednesday and Misty Morning reside in Lexington, Kentucky.

Tiger cats are called:

Tiger	Stripes
Tiger Lily	Bars
Pin Stripe	Zebra

Cats with feet of a different color are called:

Bootsie	Slippers
Mittens	Sneakers
Socks	Galoshes
Gaiters	Wellingtons

Cats with bright eyes are called:

Twinkle	Sparkle Plenty
Sparkle	Diamond Lil
Buttons	Stardust

Cats with a patch of a different color over one eye might be called:

Patches	Long John
Patchwork	Captain Hook
Pirate	Moishe Dayan

Calico cats have such pretty multicolored markings they can be named Mottle and Splash and Muffin, or named after flowers like Marigold, Pansy, Petunia, Peony and Iris. There are many more flower names to choose from further on in the book.

Cats who walk in a funny way are sometimes named for the way they walk. A Kentucky cat who lost his foot when he was little and hops along on three legs and a stump is called Hopalong. Another cat who can't walk straight because of an illness that affected his nervous system is called Sideways. One who dips a little as he walks is called Dips-A-Little. Waddles waddles. And a cat in Pennsylvania is called Grasshopper because he used to hop like one when he was a kitten.

※⁑ↂↈ⁑※

If you are more tuned in to the audio section of your cat than the visual . . .

Rhum-Rhum is named after the gentle sound of his purr. Evinrude, who summered on Fire Island with his nine-year-old mistress, purred like her outboard motor. A similar young miss calls her cat Motorboat. If I had a cat with a deep, growly, explosive purr I'd call him Harley Davidson. Or Norton, or Honda, or Yamaha, or Kawasaki.

※⁑ↂↈ⁑※

There are those who take a larger view of the matter and take into account not only the audio/visual aspects of their cat, but also some additional traits of character that remind them of someone they know.

※⁑ↂↈ⁑※

In Berlin in the '30s a boy grew up in a big, elegant house. His family was rich and cultured, and important people came and went about his home. There lived with the family an elderly relative whose name was Uncle Gustav. Uncle Gustav was large and fat and blind and spent most of his days snoring gently in a comfortable armchair. But large and fat and blind and asleep as he mostly was, nothing went on in that house that escaped Uncle Gustav's attention.

There came a time, when the boy was about ten, that his life was in danger because he was in part Jewish. He had to be hidden, and in Berlin this was no easy matter. But because he was a mathematical genius and his family well-connected, he was hidden in a famous Institute of Science on the outskirts of the city, and there his toys were the most advanced experimental weapons of the day. He survived, and many years later in another country a cat walked into his home and stayed. The cat is large and fat and spends most of his days curled up in an armchair, eyes closed, snoring gently, and nothing that goes on in the house escapes his notice. His name is Uncle Gustav.

Don't worry if you don't have an interesting relative or friend. And don't worry if you don't have a name for your cat after a week or even a month. Given the life expectancy of a well-looked-after cat these days, you are about to embark on a long-term relationship that may well outlast your marriage. In all probability you're looking at fifteen years of love and laughter, so it makes sense at the beginning to take time to relax together. Only then will your cat display those subtler aspects of his character that might be most nameworthy, and only then will you be able to tune in to them.

A new cat, depending on his background, may need several days or weeks or even months to adjust to his new home. The more secure his kittenhood or the conditions of his life before he moved in with you, the sooner he'll feel at home. Conversely, a disadvantaged cat needs more time, attention and reassurance.

⁂

Talk, touch and play are the best ways to develop an intimate relationship. It's no great strain to have a conversation with a cat. Greet him when you come home in the evening, ask him how his day has been and tell him about yours. Or pick him up in your arms and talk nonsense. Cats are adept at understanding the nuances in the human voice. They love to be talked to and most cats love to be touched. You could recite the alphabet or your laundry list and they'd be happy. I dare say they wouldn't mind if you groused about the traffic jam, or the crush in the subway, or the rising cost of living. You will feel more relaxed if you unburden yourself, the cat will respond to your relaxation, and you, in turn, will respond to the cat's.

Cuddle your cat. Touch gives reassurance and pleasure to you both—and it may save your life!

A science program telecast on public television cited a British study of the backgrounds of people who had survived major heart surgery and found that the single factor common to all who had survived was the ownership of a pet. The study concluded that touch, physical contact, the frequent and often unconscious stroking of the pet may have been the most significant ingredient of all. Similar studies in this country have recently confirmed these findings. In addition, experimental programs in our prisons have shown that there is markedly less tension and violence among even the most hardened criminals when they are allowed to have a pet of their own in their cells. In fact these convicted felons, among whom can be counted armed robbers, rapists and murderers, have reported greater feelings of relaxation and well-being since having their pets.

So, felon or no, stroke your cat. Stroke his whiskers, scratch gently under his chin and behind his ears, run your hands along the length of his back, pull gently on his quivering tail and when he rolls over, rub his tummy tenderly.

Brush his coat regularly with long, firm strokes. Most cats love this rhythmic stroking; it probably reminds them of their mother washing them. I used to keep a brush for this purpose in one of the many drawers of a manufacturer's oak file chest I used as a coffee table. If I opened any drawer at all as I sat there in the evening, my Dolly would rush forward, all agog and tail aquiver in anticipation. As I brushed her, she purred in ecstasy, and Humphrey and Bean Blossom would stand in line for their turn. So I'd brush Dolly for a few minutes, then turn to Humphrey and brush him for a few minutes, then Bean Blossom, then Dolly again and so on, up and down the line, producing a most harmonious chorus of purrs. They'd be so turned on I'd get out their wind-up toy mice and their soft rubber balls, and soon there would be mechanical mice going in all directions and balls bouncing every which way, and cats leaping around the room like ballet dancers. Sometimes I would tie a long piece of ribbon to a cork and stand in a clear space and twirl it around me as though I were a Maypole.

Not even the most elderly and curmudgeonly of cats could resist and this is a wonderful way to entice a timid cat from under the sofa or to introduce a new cat to the other cats in the family.

With kittens it is especially delightful to get down to their level and romp on the floor. Whenever I had transient kittens, I loved to put down a tray of food for them, then stretch out beside them and watch them eat. When they had eaten, they would race along my legs and play cowboys and Indians around my feet. If I'd brought along a pillow we would all stretch out, them on my tummy, purring and gently heaving together. Cat naps are not only for cats.

By interacting with your cat in this way, you should soon have some clues to the broad outlines of his personality. Is he:

timid or bold?
sweet-natured or grumpy?
calm or frenetic?
lethargic or energetic?
fastidious or messy?
introverted or extroverted?
affectionate or aloof?
dependent or independent?
demanding or undemanding?
discreet or rushing in where angels fear to tread?

Maybe your cat seems to possess all these qualities on different days of the week. Fret not! Sooner or later you will notice that certain traits predominate. Now this is where your personality comes into it. The characteristics in your cat that you tune in to will say as much about you as your cat. Perhaps the feline qualities most apparent to you are part of your own makeup, or maybe they're qualities you find lacking in yourself and wish you had. Maybe you think of yourself as timid and respond protectively to the timidity in your cat, or admiringly to his boldness. Whichever way it goes, once you have zeroed in on some characteristics that seem central to your cat's personality, your mind will begin to hunt around for names that *you* associate with these characteristics.

※♥○♥彡

Humphrey, Dolly and Bean Blossom got their names in the following way. They were born to a mother cat whose only home was a doorstep by a warm chimney stack in one of the yards behind my apartment. I first saw them from the bedroom window playing in a nearby garden in the moonlight, and when I learned from a neighbor that the cat's kittens usually died in winter, I made up my mind to rescue them. I gained access to the garden and by dint of lying in wait and a great deal of running around—for they were wild—I finally caught all three. Once caught, the gray and white female was quite bold, but the two little males trembled with fear, so I made a bed for them all in the bathroom, where they lived for a week till they got accustomed to my feeding and touching them.

The first to be named was the gray and white kitten, and that took several weeks of trying names on for size. She was a bold, practical kitten, quick on the uptake. She soon learned her way around the apartment, large as it was, and taking the boys under her wing, showed them the ropes. She had a way of managing her brothers and events around her that rang a bell when I saw the character Dolly Levy in the musical *Hello, Dolly!* And Dolly she was.

The second to be named was the orange and white kitten. I had read in *The New Yorker* about a group of school children from the little town of Bean Blossom, Indiana, who were visiting the city for the first time. They rode the subways and walked around the streets wide-eyed, necks craning at the tall buildings, some a bit bewildered by it all. I was intrigued by the article since I had arrived in New York from a small Scottish village just a few years before with much the same reaction. I pictured a Bean Blossom as an orange and white flower and when my small orange and white kitten began to explore the apartment, eyes wide with wonder and neck craning upward at the giant furniture and skyscraper people, something clicked inside me; the association was made and henceforth he was Bean Blossom.

I'm going to digress at this point because it suits my purpose. After the kittens settled in, I rented a trap from the A.S.P.C.A. to catch the mother cat, who was wild, and have her spayed. When her stitches were removed and her incision healed, I put her back in the alley and fed her regularly over the winter, throwing liver and kidneys and chicken (bones removed) from my kitchen window, which was on the side of the building. The following spring I opened up the rear window of my bedroom, hitherto sealed shut, and there where the brownstone gardens met the backs of the tenements was my destiny: more new faces, more mouths to be fed, more kittens to be rescued. My then husband put down his foot, said that three was the limit of his tolerance and the rest had better be on their way to other homes. What chance did I have? Not only was I spiritually unadvanced, my ego was weak and I was a recent immigrant to boot. I accepted the rule. In somewhat the same manner as my Presbyterian forebears who journeyed to the far corners of the Empire to save the souls of heathens, I found that, unsuspecting, I had come to America to embark upon the calling of saving the lives of cats and kittens. Sometimes I used to feel like the woman who lived in a shoe: I had so many kittens to find homes for, I didn't know what to do. Being an artists' agent in those days, I took up the practice of making my rounds of publishing houses and advertising agencies with a portfolio under one arm and a carrier full of kittens under the other.

It took no time at all to discover that the more inspired their names, the quicker they were adopted, and when I was low on inspiration I wrote résumés describing their personalities and the particulars of their lives and left them on bulletin boards all over town. In doing this I came to realize that, while each cat was an individual, like human beings they could be fitted into personality categories that influenced my choice of names. Clearly these categories reflect my view of humans as well as cats, but you may find them useful and you may want to add a few of your own.

Categories of Cats

GALLANTS

Now back to my third kitten, the gray one. It took many weeks to find a name for him. I hadn't had kittens since childhood and I had no thought in those days of categorizing cats, but I took my time and enjoyed him. His personality was subtler than his siblings', my relationship with him was more complex and, looking back, I see I loved him best of all my cats. In choosing his name I had unconscious associations that I continued to be unaware of for a long time. After discarding many other possibilities that were close but no cigar, one day I just knew his name was Humphrey. I got a lot of satisfaction from saying it aloud and a glow of pleasure from just thinking about it. Many years went by before I realized I'd named him after Hubert Horatio Humphrey, the senator from Minnesota. In those days, HHH was often on television and I developed an affection for him. I liked his round, gentle, jovial face, his optimism, his goodwill and his persistent championing of social justice. My gray kitten's face was round and his manner also gentle. He was as playful as any kitten, but in repose, like HHH, he had a certain dignity and gravity of manner, enhanced by the markings of his gray striped suit. But beyond the apparent was a quality I sensed unconsciously in both: the knight in shining armor, the bold Sir Galahad. I wasn't aware then that I needed a

protector and I most certainly wasn't aware that I was looking for one in this small gray kitten, so recently trembling in
fear, but it surfaced several years later when I was startled
by the water bug and called out involuntarily, *"Humphrey,
save me!"*

Apart from any personal heroes you may have, the most
notable gallants are the Knights of the Round Table:

King Arthur	Sir Perceval
Sir Galahad	Sir Bedivere
Sir Launcelot	Sir Gareth
Sir Tristram	Sir Geraint
Sir Pelleas	Sir Balin
Sir Gawain	Sir Balan

Other heroes from my childhood are:

Lochinvar	Ivanhoe
Jock O'Hazeldean	Robin Hood
Robert the Bruce	Richard the Lionheart
Bonnie Dundee	El Cid
Rob Roy MacGregor	Prince Gruffydd of Gwynedd
Bonnie Prince Charlie	Owen Glendower
William Wallace	Judah Ben-Hur

ARISTOCRATS

In appearance and personality some cats are clearly aristocratic if not outright royal. The air of haughtiness, fastidiousness and refinement is unmistakable. Elegant-limbed Siamese with startling blue eyes and Persians with luxuriously flowing fur and magnificent ruffs demand recognition of their grandeur. Sometimes the names of kings, queens, emperors, empresses, princes, dukes, grand duchesses and folks of that ilk seem most suitable. Here are some aristos noteworthy in their day.

Pharaoh	Henry VIII and Anne Boleyn
Aminhotep	Good Queen Bess
Tutankhamen	Mary, Queen of Scots
Solomon and Sheba	Queen Anne
Olympias	Queen Christina
Nefertiti	Catherine the Great
Ptolemy	Henri Quatre
Cleopatra	Louis Seize
Augustus and Livia	Marie Antoinette
Justinian and Theodora	Napoleon and Josephine
Harun al-Rashid	Ludwig
Charles the Fat	Maximilian
Charles the Simple	Maria Theresa
Charles the Good	Franz Joseph
Wenceslas	Victoria and Albert
Harold Bluetooth	Nicholas and Alexandra
Edgar the Peaceful	Olga
King Rajaraja	Tatiana
Henry the Proud	Anastasia
Eric the Saint	Wilhelmina
Tamara, Queen of Georgia	Juliana
Alfonso the Wise	George and Mary
Philip the Fair	Elizabeth Regina
Lorenzo the Magnificent	Margaret Rose
Lucrezia Borgia	Charles and Diana
Philip the Handsome	Prince Andrew

But your cat doesn't have to be a thoroughbred to qualify for this category. A good coat and a haughty manner will get anyone in, as in life itself. Comportment is all, delusions of grandeur an asset. Consider Sophie.

Sophie was a duchess. There was no mistaking her rank, though she had been found wailing in a tenement hallway when she was a kitten and lived in a tenement all her life. She was a short-haired multicolored cat whose tones were dusty and muted in a laid-back, rich kind of way. She had a long, lean, elegant body and an expanse of ermine around her throat and neck. She slept on a velvet pillow, which in summer was covered with the finest Egyptian cotton, and beside it was a box containing her toys. Her veal kidneys were always warmed to room temperature and if by chance she was served food from a can, it was spooned out with a two-hundred-year-old silver spoon onto a little gray crackle plate with a border of blue bunny rabbits. Her manner with company was reserved to say the least; in the fifteen years I knew her she rarely responded to my blandishments.

My cat William has an orange patch over one eye that might be rakish in another cat. But William has an otherworldly air, an inward, musing, dreamy quality. He has aesthetic sensibilities; he loves fresh-cut flowers and sniffs them gently, clearly intending them no harm, and often curls up asleep around the vase containing them. His particular passion is carnations. Sometimes I've risen in the morning to find a dozen of them removed from their water and lined up on the table next to their vase. William is fastidious in his eating habits and very sensitive to nuances of tone in the human voice; he can spot a quarrel brewing long before I can, and discreetly leaves the room before it starts. On occasion he can also read your mind. Don't imagine, however, you can push this cat around. Don't ever try to put his back against the wall, for William has a slender core of steel. William is a match for any cat. William is a mighty hunter and a good provider. When we lived in an apartment with a terrace that looked up at the stars and the Hotel Pierre, William brought us gifts of giant water bugs wriggling in his mouth, which he thoughtfully stashed under the living room carpet against the day of our need.

Of poets named William, the most famous are Shakespeare, Wordsworth and Blake.

And . . .

Homer	Percy Bysshe Shelley
Hesiod	Lord Byron
Virgil	Browning
Horace	Rudyard Kipling
Ovid	Alfred, Lord Tennyson
Mutanabi	Oscar Wilde
Omar Khayam	Siegfried Sassoon
Taliesin	Yeats
Chaucer	T. S. Eliot
Dunbar	Ezra
Marlowe	Dylan
Lovelace	Burns
John Donne	MacDiarmid
Milton	Abelard

Keats
François Villon
Verlaine
Rimbaud
La Fontaine
Petrarch
Tasso
Dante
Goethe
Rilke
Tannhäuser
Snorri Sturluson
Pushkin
Pasternak
Yevtushenko
Whitman
Longfellow
Edgar Allan Poe
Sandburg
Frost

Ronsard
Hart Crane
Countee Cullen
Delmore
Randall Jarrell
Arna Bontemps
Ashbery
Sappho
Christina Georgina Rossetti
Elizabeth Barrett Browning
Sylvia Townsend Warner
Edna St. Vincent Millay
Emily Dickinson
Sara Teasdale
Marianne Moore
Hilda Doolittle
Cornelia Meigs
Sylvia Plath
Mayakovska

And don't forget Anonymous . . .

SEXPOTS

These cats are very self-assured. They know they have sex appeal and they use it to get their way.

The female is a pretty, provocative creature who arches her back and swishes her tail alluringly and makes a beeline for the nearest male lap. There she lies langorously while she is petted and stroked, purring sensuously, gazing with rapture into the eyes of the besotted man who smirks and looks around in hopes that this preference for him is being witnessed by all. And if baby lamb chops are being served for supper, guess who will get half of his.

The male is lithe and well-muscled. He'll woo you unabashedly, lounging on the back of the sofa, paws entwined around your neck, nibbling your ear lobes, teasing strands of your hair.

Antonio was such a cat. He was named after a Latin lover of his mistress and behaved accordingly. He had bedroom eyes and his coat was short and smooth as silk. His muscles rippled and he walked with a hint of a swagger, like a young Marlon Brando. He knew which side his bed was buttered on and romanced his mistress shamelessly, throwing his lithe young body against hers, tail vibrating with ecstasy. When she went to bed at night, he would rub his whiskers against her cheek, insinuate himself under her armpit and gaze into her eyes in apparent adoration. One could not hope for a more ardent swain. And, true to form, when his mistress goes out of town and her friend Katerina comes to stay, Antonio woos her just as zealously as he ever did his true love, the moment she picks up the can opener.

Give sexy cats names that seem sexy to you. You can name females after exotic, heavy-scented or opulent flowers like Jasmine, Magnolia, Orchid, Dahlia, Honeysuckle, Camelia. Or after famous sex symbols like:

Salome	Jane Russell
Jezebel	Marilyn Monroe
Delilah	Brigitte Bardot
Messallina	La Lollo
Madame du Barry	Sophia

Mata Hari   Sylvana Mangano
Pola Negri   Raquel Welch
Lulu   Farrah Fawcett
Harlow   Morgan Fairchild
Veronica Lake   Brooke
Rita Hayworth   Bo
Lana Turner   Christie

For sexy males I like names with a macho ring like Ace, Bailey, Ben, Beau, Harlan. And:

Valentino   Brando
Fairbanks   Newman and Redford
Alan Ladd   Poitier and Belafonte
Johnny Weismuller   Marcello Mastroianni
Kirk Douglas   Sean Connery
Gable   Langella
Rock Hudson   Christopher Reeve
Charlton   Travolta and Stallone
Omar Sharif

For a sexy couple, Liz and Dick.

These are sensible, reliable cats, possessed of discretion and common sense. They are seldom in the wrong place at the wrong time and never embarrass you in front of friends. They are empathetic and usually very cooperative. Often they are the plainer pumpkins of the litter whose sweetness of disposition will steal your heart. Such a one was Polly Flinders, a small, plain, gray and white kitten in a batch of beauties. Her coloration and markings were nondescript but her heart was pure gold and her love beyond rubies. I found her sitting, like the little girl in the nursery rhyme, among the cinders in my hearth one morning while her siblings lay asleep in their wicker house. Of course I didn't spank her, but as I bathed her I explained gently that it would be a nuisance to both of us to go through this process every day, and she listened carefully and never did it again. She loved to romp with her brothers and sisters but the moment I lay on the bed, she'd be up and nestling under my chin, purring boisterously, her nose pressed to mine, her pink tongue gently scouring my cheeks.

Like my Dolly, practical cats seem especially capable of logical thought. In that brownstone apartment where we first lived, there were two fireplaces. Both had hearths with logs placed in them, but only one was in working condition, the chimney of the other being boarded up. One afternoon there was a hailstorm; big hailstones came down the open chimney and bounced off the unlit logs. Dolly was fascinated and stood with her forepaws on the logs, gazing up the chimney in wonder. Ten minutes later I saw her in the other room, forepaws on the decorative birch logs, gazing up that chimney in hopeful expectation. Watching her, I could see her hope turn to disappointment and after a few minutes she walked away with a thoughtful, puzzled look on her face.

I like practical names for practical cats:

Mabel	Martha
Harriet	Mavis
Bridget	Edith
Mary-Margaret	Louise

Mildred
Hilda
Dora
Lizzie
Ruth
Penelope
Lucy
Muriel

Phyllis
Nellie
Molly
Hester
Dolores
Elsie
Jane

For the practical male:

Max
Harry
George
Jim
Peter
Harold
Gilbert
Stanley
Monty

Fletcher
Ginsberg
Murphy
Joe
Sam
Roger
Chester
Neddy
Charlie

NAUGHTY, WICKED CATS
(OR MISCHIEF WITH MALICE AFORETHOUGHT)

There are some cats whose sense of timing is so acute that after a while you begin to suspect their acts of mischief are premeditated. There's an intelligence and will at work and despite your many kindnesses and considerations, it's frequently at work against you.

My black velvet cat, Amagansett, has eyes as green as gooseberries and two long fangs like Count Dracula's protruding from his upper jaw. Butter would not melt in his mouth. He blew three homes in his kittenhood; each returned him with assurances that there was no fault in the kitten and vague references to "circumstances" that no longer permitted . . . Unsuspecting, I took him on as a permanent member of the household when Bean Blossom died. I cannot say I have lived to regret it; he is a warm-hearted, affectionate creature and very kind to kittens. But I have learned to watch out. This is just one of his exploits:

By this time my beloved brownstone was reduced to rubble and we had moved grudgingly to an apartment on lower Fifth Avenue, where late one afternoon I was preparing the final stages of dinner for six. Half an hour before my guests arrived, furniture and floor glowing, the table set, the main course in hand, I embarked upon a spinach salad. Fresh spinach, as you and Amagansett well know, must be washed at least seven times in icy water to remove the grit, a tedious chore at best and one in which a cheerful companion eases the pain. Amagansett seated himself on the counter to the left of the kitchen sink, watching me wash and wash again mountains of green spinach till my fingers were numb with cold. He looked on with sympathy and understanding, following every movement. The next step was to spin the spinach dry in a salad basket, which I did on the service stairs outside the kitchen door. Amagansett beseeched me to let him accompany me, lest I be lonely, and sat steadfastly by me as I whirled the basket over my head at arm's length. It took a lot of whirling to get rid of the excess water, but finally we were satisfied and went back into the kitchen for

stage three. Stage three called for patting each leaf of spinach dry with a fresh bath towel. Amagansett again sat cheerfully on the counter to the left of the sink, watching carefully as I patted each leaf and placed them on another towel
laid on the counter to the right of the sink, creating a sea of
green. He squeezed his eyes to narrow slits as he looked at
me, a sign of his devotion. My heart was happy. I felt lucky
to have such a faithful cat. Five minutes before my guests
were due, I turned for a fleeting moment to the cupboard
behind me and lifted down an exquisite salad bowl in which
to place my perfect greens. When I turned back I found my
true companion rolling vigorously in the spinach, all four
legs in the air and a look of glee on his face.

Good names for wicked cats are:

Machiavelli	Megaera
Iago	Tisiphone
Lucifer	Mehitabel
Nick	Tinkerbell
Mephistopheles	Puck
Beelzebub	Grendel
Sulphur	Rumpelstiltskin
Brimstone	Screwtape
Lilith	Wormwood
Circe	Quint
Setebos	Caliban
Sycorax	Caligula
Calypso	Nero
Broom Hilda	Sejanus
Alecto	Krum

CAPTAINS OF INDUSTRY

These are sleek, well-fed cats with a self-important air and ponderous manners. They move with slow deliberation and their confidence is manifest. They are Chairmen of the Board, decision makers, who are not above cuffing you on the ear if you overstep the line, and they don't like retiring from their positions of authority. They have a good head for finance and an uncanny ability to plan ahead. In New York they generally live on Park Avenue.

Fanshaw was an imposing cat of portly dimensions. He had a tendency to lengthy conversation and could hold forth for hours on any subject you sought his opinion on. He had a mind of his own and firm ideas about comportment. If asked to do something he considered beneath his dignity, he would stare his mistress coldly in the eye and distinctly say *No*. In his middle years he became obsessed with retirement benefits and would pick up coins in his mouth and hoard them under a corner of the Oriental rug in the drawing room against the day of need. At nineteen he died a rich cat, leaving an estate with ample funds for his remains to be cremated and placed in an alabaster urn in that very drawing room, where they are to this day. And his mistress swears that every now and again, as she passes by, she still hears a faint, defiant *No* from the urn.

Such important cats need important names like:

Rutherford	Culpepper
Spencer	Wimbledon
Stanford	Travis
Benedict	Winchester
Poindexter	Fairfield
Sutton	Kirkpatrick
Winston	Wallace
Simpson	Helmsley
Porter	Woolworth
Tavistock	Livingston
Dimbleby	De Witt
Willoughby	Hofbauer
Carleton	Randolph

Templeton	Mortimer
Buckminster	Philpott
Harcourt	Matilda
Bartleby	Maude
Hildegarde	Hermione
Adelaide	Hortense
Gertrude	Euphemia
Edwina	Ernestina

TOUGH CATS

The first tough cat I met in my alley had chewed-up ears and a head the size of a cabbage. He was a battle-seasoned pro and numero uno in his domain. The other cats kept out of his way. He walked where he pleased, ate what he pleased and took female companionship whenever he pleased. I named him Bill Sykes after the rough villain of Charles Dickens's *Oliver Twist,* which was at that time a Broadway musical.

Another fierce cat I once knew ruled a packing shed down by Canal Street. I named him Attila the Hun; the ground seemed to tremble where he walked.

I've met many tough cats on the waterfronts, in warehouses and in the alleys where homeless cats gather. They're quick to lash out, move in and take over, and they die as they have lived—fighting.

But the toughest cat I've ever known is Ebony. Ebony's brother, Pierre, got a good home on Long Island, but Ebony was kept to be a companion to his mother, Baby, a large black cat who lives in the shop of Domenick the TV repairman. However, Baby very soon had another litter of kittens and slapped and hissed at Ebony when he wanted to suckle her too. Ebony was understandably upset. Indeed, he was traumatized by his mother's rejection. Domenick took him upstairs to his apartment where he was the only cat, and, to console him, played with Ebony as much as he could, covering his arm with a jacket and teaching the cat to attack as though he were a German shepherd. Ebony, undoubtedly nurturing rage toward his mother, took the games to heart and now attacks anyone who sets foot in Domenick's apartment, leaping from the ground and drawing blood with his claws. While this was not Domenick's intention, Ebony was clearly better than a burglar alarm, and on hot summer evenings Domenick would leave his apartment door open for cross ventilation while Ebony sat guard on the hallway stairs refusing to let anyone pass without Domenick's consent. The other tenants of the building soon got used to this, figuring Ebony was a crime deterrent, and would call out, "Hey, Domenick. Call off the cat!"

One evening Domenick heard angry voices outside his open door and looking out he found Ebony facing down two policemen, one of whom had finally drawn his gun on the cat who refused to back off even from New York's finest.

Names I like for tough cats are:

Dogbane	Warfarin
Ratsbane	Kong
Sweeney Todd	Luigi
Captain Bligh	Ugolini
Otto	Sparafucile
Igor	Warlord
Frankenstein	Warpaint
Ratrap	

You can also name tough cats after gangsters such as:

Bugsy Siegel	Ma Barker
Pretty Boy Floyd	Bonnie Parker
Dutch Schultz	Clyde Barrow
Legs Diamond	Lucky Luciano
John Dillinger	Frank Costello
Bugs Moran	Meyer Lansky
Machine Gun Kelly	Al Capone

And after tough guys of yesteryear:

Zoser	Henry the Quarrelsome
Lugalzaggisi	Sancho the Great
Sargon	Robert the Devil
Solon	Macbeth
Nebuchadnezzar	William the Conqueror
Xerxes	Albert the Bear
Darius	Frederick Barbarossa
Xenophon	Saladin
Samson	Charles the Bold
Hannibal	Lodovico Sforza
Julius Caesar	Ivan the Terrible
Barabbas	Akbar the Great
Zeno	Gustavus Adolphus
Charlemagne	Peter the Great
Genghis Khat	Frederick the Great
Kublai Khat	Prince Potëmkin

That's enough of categories, for no matter how fine and funny they may be, cats are often so subtle they elude categorization, and humans are often so perverse that even though a cat may fit a category, we balk at being logical and choose a name from left field. If categorizing leaves you cold, you might cast around for a name in one of your interests or obsessions.

If you've secretly hankered to be a doctor you could call your cat Stethoscope; if paleontology is your passion you could call your cat Diplodocus; if you are a war buff you could name your cat after a famous battle like Bull Run, Iwo Jima or Culloden.

A french horn player married a violinist and they had four kittens, whom they called Pizzicato, Pianissimo, Oboe and Piccolo.

The world is your oyster. . . .

Sources of Names

THE GARDEN

Not every flower name is suitable for a cat—Hydrangea, Gladiola and Scabiosa lack that certain something. Others will do charmingly:

Snapdragon	Daisy
Jonquil	Morning Glory
Daffodil	Dusty Miller
Poppy	Pickerel
Pansy	Arathusa
Petunia	Ladybell
Jasmine	Foxfire
Sweet Pea	Sapodilla
Iris	Japonica
Lily	Caliopsis
Dandelion	Milkweed
Honeysuckle	Dogbane
Marigold	Butterwort
Hyacinth	Buttercup
Lilac	Rose
Magnolia	Lotus
Columbine	Baby's-breath
Cuckoo-bud	Larkspur
Primrose	Mariposa
Gillyvor	Oleander

Peony	Chrysanthemum
Impatiens	Thistledown
Forget-Me-Not	Harebell

Even the humble vegetable garden will yield some good cat names as will your neighborhood fruit stand. Rutabaga is my favorite.

Asparagus	Quince
Artichoke	Pomegranate
Zucchini	Persimmon
Pokeweed	Kiwi
Okra	Banana
Beetroot	Apple
Cabbage	Strawberry
Chickpea	Raspberry
Turnip	Watermelon
Cauliflower	Casaba
Squash Blossom	Lemon
Eggplant	Lime
Spinach	Rhubarb
Arugula	Salsify
Beansprout	Succotash
Alfalfa	

And don't forget herbs and spices. For a quartet of kittens: Parsley, Sage, Rosemary and Thyme.

Basil	Ginger
Fennel	Clove
Chervil	Cumin
Pennyroyal	Oregano
Peppermint	Tarragon
Cinnamon	Marjoram
Nutmeg	Dill

THE SUPERMARKET

Two little girls in Frankfort, Kentucky, got a cat. After giving the matter a lot of thought they decided to call her Campbell's Soup, and when her kittens came along they were named Chicken Noodle, Minestrone, Gumbo and Vegetable Beef.

Walk around your local supermarket and look at the items on the shelves and think of them not as food but as cats' names.

I like:

Alka-Seltzer	Mott
Ultrabrite	Heinz
Kosher	Sunsweet
Cashew	Kellogg
Peanut	Nabisco
Chunky	Ovaltine
Skippy	Macaroni
Pepperidge	Grits
Swanson	Farina
Lipton	Granola
Cadbury	Pickles
Chivers	Relish
Marmalade	Jell-O
Dickinson	Pudding
Jalapeno	Sardine
Morton	Goober
Twining	Olive
Hershey	Coke
Maxwell	Pepsi
Ronzoni	Palmolive
Pillsbury	Ajax
Flako	Ivory
Crisco	Joy
Jiffy	Rinso
Domino	Brillo
Jemima	Bounty
Libby	Viva
Delmonte	

THE AUTOMOBILE

There was a young man from Ohio who spent all his spare
time tinkering with his car, taking it apart, laying it out all
over the yard, cleaning the individual parts, putting it all
together again. And as soon as it was finished, or so it seemed,
he'd start all over again. Early in the game a young cat, clearly
male, strolled into the yard, inspected the work and settled
down in its midst with an approving purr. Every day, as soon
as the work began, the cat appeared, showing a serious in-
terest in its progress. Pretty soon he was accepting the offer
of half a sandwich and a sip of beer. This continued for some
time till all of a sudden one day it became apparent to both
parties that this was a permanent liaison by mutual consent.
His name is Axle.

Rearaxle	Hood
Hubcap	Mag Wheels
Sparkplug	Whitewall
Grease	Spokes
Crankshaft	Alfa Romeo
Flywheel	Ferrari
Piston	Bugatti
Jack	Triumph
Tubeless	MG
Backfire	Rolls
Dipstick	Mercedes
Tailpipe	Daimler
Muffler	Porsche
Trade In	Rabbit
Windshield	Edsel
Choke	Ford
Carburetor	Chevy

THE MOVIES

If I had a dollar for every kitten in these United States whose
name is E.T., I'd be a rich woman.

Han Solo	McCabe and Mrs. Miller
Luke Skywalker	Marjorie Morningstar
Leia Organa	Suzie Wong
Yoda	Sophie
R2D2	Nathan
C3PO	Stingo
Obi-Wan Kenobi	Mrs. Miniver
Chewbacca	Trilby and Svengali
Wicket	Breathless
Lando Calrissian	Serpico
Darth Vader	Shampoo
Jabba the Hutt	Sleeper
Indiana Jones	Butch Cassidy
Godfather I	Sundance
Godfather II	Rocky I
James Bond	Rocky II
007	Rocky III
Dr. No	Barbarosa
Goldfinger	Outland
Thunderball	The Sisters Gish
Pussy Galore	Garbo
Scarlett O'Hara	Dietrich
Rhett Butler	Ida Lupino
Ashley Wilkes	Howard Duff
Melanie	Nelson and Jeannette
Aunt Pitty Pat	Bogart and Bacall
Mildred Pierce	Ingrid
Annie Hall	Claude
Cutter	Tracy and Hepburn
Zelig	Greer
Cimarron	Heddy
Shane	Broderick Crawford
Tootsie	Mercedes
Deliverance	Maria Montez
Resurrection	Davis and Crawford
Georgie Girl	Maria Ouspenskaya
Funnyface	Boris
Sidney Greenstreet	Cissy

Belushi and Ackroyd

Treat

Dustin

Streep

Woodward and Newman

Tarzan and Jane

TELEVISION

Good Morning, America
Dr. Snuggles
Uncle Floyd
Chico and The Man
Superfriend
Heckle and Jeckle
Popeye and Olive Oyl
Fraggle Rock
Footsteps
Startrek
Nova
Thundarr
Love Boat
Crossfire
Livewire
Hill Street Blue
Dallas
Dynasty
Saturday Night Live
Sanford
Mary Tyler Moore
Oral Roberts
Little Rascal
John Boy
J.R.
S.W.A.T.
Roseanne Roseannadanna
Kool and The Gang
Pinwheel
Our Times
Groovie Goolies
Night Flight
Tattletale
Flickers
Captain Bob
Quincy
Rockford

Donahue
Rhoda
Monty Python
Batman and Robin
Buck Rogers
Hogan
Alice
Trapper John
Magnum
Maude
Starsky and Hutch
Mork and Mindy
Laverne and Shirley
Bat Masterson
Gunsmoke
Hazel
Paladin
Julia Child
Emma Peel
Mr. Steed
Napoleon Solo
Ilya Kuryakin
Upstairs and Downstairs
Poldark
Thika
Lord and Lady Bellamy
Huntley and Brinkley
Cronkite and Sevareid
MacNeil and Lehrer
Agronsky
Roger Mudd
Barbara Walters
Liberace, George and Mom
Hawkeye
Radar
Potter
Hot Lips Houlihan

Billards

Minnesota Fats and Fast Eddie, the two most famous pool hustlers in the world, are figments of the literary imagination in the novel *The Hustler*. Fats and Eddie would be great names for a fat cat and a fast cat if you had that particular combination.

More names from the real world of pool are:

Willie Mosconi
Cornbread Red
Tobacco Red
Machine Gun Lou
Flyboy
The Preacher
The Knoxville Bear
The Tennessee Tarzan
Detroit Whitey
Boston Shorty
Youngblood
The Shufala Kid

Weenie Beenie
Hawaiian Brian
One-Eyed Tony
Toupée Jay
The Meatman
The Rifleman
Captain Hook
Cicero Murphy
Wimpy Lassiter
St. Louie Louie
Little David

Chess

Capablanca
Morphy
Alekhine
Lasker
Petrov
Tal
Korchnoi
Karpov
Borgov
Spassky
Petrosian
Nimzo
Mengarini
Bogolyubov
Boleslavski
Ponziani
Falkbeer

Philidor
Opocensky
Reti
Benoni
Fegatello
Pirc
Levenfish
Szabo
Trompovsky
Rossolimo
Maroczy
Ruy Lopez
Bobby Fischer
Fianchetto
En Passant
Gardez

Bridge

If you like bridge you might consider naming your cat after one of the members of the spectacular Italian Blue Team, which won ten consecutive world championships and three consecutive Team Olympiads in the late fifties and early sixties. The principal players at the end of this reign were:

Benito Garozzo   Walter Avarelli
Pietro Forquet   Massimo D'Alelio
Giorgio Belladonna   Camillo Pabis Ticci

Baseball

Once in the subway on the way to see my therapist I saw the word *Mookie* screaming at me from the back page of a newspaper. When I got off I checked it out at the corner newsstand—*Mookie Wilson* of the New York Mets—entered it in my Cat Names Notebook and went on to my therapist, where I was cheerfully greeted by the preceding patient, exiting as I was entering. She was a friend whom I hadn't seen in a year, as is often the way in New York, and she looked radiant.

"I finally got my new cat," she said. There had been trouble getting it across the border from Canada, where it was born.

"Boy or girl?" I asked.

"Boy."

"What's its name?"

"Mookie."

"Mookie Wilson?"

"The same."

This betokened emotional growth of an encouraging nature. My friend had been a solitary though beautiful young woman who had lived alone for several years with her previous cat, significantly named Hamlet. Then she married a young man with two roustabout cats, Bert and Mumphy (one of whom I'd rescued from under a pile of scrap metal near Canal Street) and they all lived together in a very small apartment. Hamlet, as solitary by nature as the Dane himself, went quite mad. His mistress fared better than Ophelia but no one emerged unscathed, although they were all good people and good cats. They went their separate ways, and time and commitment to growth healed their wounds.

More good cat names from baseball:

Rookie	Enos Slaughter
Shortstop	Whitey Kurowski
Umpire	Frankie Frisch
Vida Blue	George Munger
Sparky Lyle	Red Schoendienst
Valenzuela	Pepper Martin
Babe Ruth	Hank Aaron
Jackie Robinson	Darrell Porter
Willie Mays	Willie McGee
Joe DiMaggio	Ozzie Smith
Ty Cobb	Cecil Cooper
Napoleon Lajoie	Rollie Fingers
Lefty O'Doul	Claudell Washington
Joe Garagiola	Hubie Brooks
Cookie Lavagetto	Ellis Valentine
Elrod Hendricks	Reggie Jackson

Football

When I next get hold of a handsome, athletic, young hunk of a cat I believe I'll call him Prince McJunkins III.

O. J. Simpson	Dante Lavelli
Joe Willie Namath	Marion Motley
Roland Hooks	Shafer Suggs
Y. A. Tittle	Frenchie Faqua
Jim Brown	Freeman McNeil
Mercury Morris	The Streak
Red Conkright	Chip Glass

Basketball

Goose Tatum	Doctor Dunk
Meadowlark Lemon	Artis
Earl the Pearl	World B. Free
Dean the Dream	Karim Abdul-Jabbar
Doctor J	Uwe Blab
The Iceman	

Tennis

Gorgeous Gussie
Rosie Casals
Althea
Billie Jean
Goolagong
Navratilova
Raponi Longo

Bjorn Borg
Pancho Gonzales
Arthur Ashe
Rosewall
McEnroe
Wilander

THE EARTH

Amagansett was found in an abandoned shopping cart in a seldom-used paint shed in an alley off lower Fifth Avenue. Even as a kitten he had a quality about him as impenetrable as the name of the little village in the Long Island dunes where I'd just spent the summer, and so he was named.

Hudson was named after the Hudson River from which he had been fished, half drowned and with a broken leg. Wallstreet is so called because his mistress works in a brokerage firm there. Ten Broeck was named after his young master's favorite shoe store in Rhinebeck, New York.

If you like New York City you could name your cat after a section of town such as:

Harlem   Chelsea
Brooklyn   Broadway
Beekman   Murray Hill
Sutton   SoHo
Gracie   NoHo
Patchin   Turtle Bay
Pomander   Kips Bay
Gramercy   Rose Hill
Stuyvesant

The writer James Tiptree, Jr., wrote to ask if I'd included her cat named Madison-Avenue-at-64th-Street, which is exactly where she rescued a poor little kitten being hit with a broom by a dreadful German doorman, in the slush of January.

If you love San Francisco, you could name your cat Frisco, or after one of that city's fabled streets:

Stanyan   Turk
Divisadero   Potrero
Vallejo   Folsom
Geary   Castro
Lombard   Sacramento
O'Farrel   Vandewater

Or you can name your cat after an American city:

Denver   Memphis
Nashville   Chattanooga

Knoxville
Atlanta
Savannah
Tampa
Tallahassee
Woodstock
Cleveland
Detroit
Jackson
Montgomery
Charleston
Shreveport
Cincinnati
Saginaw
Madison
Wichita
Topeka
Bismarck

Omaha
Dallas
Austin
Houston
Albuquerque
Missoula
Cheyenne
Hailey
Portland
Tucson
Ganado
Phoenix
Reno
Tuscarora
Carmel
Monterey
Bakersfield
L.A.

Or you can name your cat after a state:

Massachusetts
Virginia
Carolina
Kentucky
Tennessee
Alabama
Mississippi
Arkansas
Missouri
Indiana
Minnesota

Dakota
Nebraska
Oklahoma
Colorado
Arizona
Wyoming
Montana
Texas
Nevada
Georgia

Or you can name your cat after interesting towns, or cities or countries or places anywhere in the world:

Peebles
Dunfermline
Dundee
Düsseldorf
Morocco
Marrakesh
Tangier

Baghdad
Samarkand
Singapore
Rangoon
Bombay
Bengal
Rawalpindi

Lucknow   Acapulco
Istanbul   Saint Tropez
Caracas   Sardinia
Rio   Salonika
Maracaibo   Sorrento
Manzanillo   Pamplona
Venezuela   Zaragosa
Vladivostok   Patagonia
Kiev   Sargasso
Archangel   Addis Ababa
Murmansk   Akasaka
Barcelona   Kinshasa
Berlin   Kilimanjaro
Budapest   Killiecrankie
Venice   Mull of Kintyre

THE STARRY HEAVENS

Sirius
Canopus
Alpha Centauri
Arcturus
Vega
Capella
Procyon
Betelgeuse
Achernar
Beta Centauri
Altair
Alpha Crucis
Aldebaran
Spica
Antares
Pollux
Fomalhaut
Beta Crucis
Zeta
Mizar
Mercury
Venus
Mars
Jupiter
Saturn
Uranus
Neptune

Pluto
Andromeda
Aquila
Aries
Auriga
Capricornus
Cassiopeia
Columba
Cygnus
Delphinus
Dorado
Hercules
Hydra
Indus
Lepus
Musca
Orion
Pavo
Pegasus
Perseus
Phoenix
Pisces
Sagittarius
Scorpius
Taurus
Yucana
Virgo

Opera

Most opera buffs have an appreciation for fine music and a well-developed sense of the melodramatic. Some of them develop a passionate attachment to their favorite singer; one I know of is so devoted to Renata Scotto that he's named his cats Renata and Scotto. Another calls her cat La Scala Milan.

For a cat who knows how to make an entrance, and who's not above throwing an occasional temper tantrum to get her way, you might choose a name like Diva or:

Maria Callas	Anna Moffo
Leontyne Price	Kiri Te Kanawa
Kirsten Flagstadt	Roberta Peters
Nellie Melba	Frederica von Stade
Rosa Ponsell	Mirella Freni
Birgit Nilsson	Montserrat Caballe
Joan Sutherland	Grace Bumbry
Bubbles Sills	Martina Arroyó

For the equivalent male:

Luciano Pavarotti	Robert Merrill
Placido Domingo	Iussi Bjorling
Enrico Caruso	Franco Corelli
Benjamino Gigli	José Carreras
Cornell MacNeil	Ermanno Mauro
Lawrence Tibbets	Ruggero Raimondo

One fine way to get names for a large litter of kittens is to name them after characters in your favorite opera:

Cio-Cio San, Madame Butterfly, Benjamin Franklin Pinkerton, Suzuki, Sharpless, Yamadori, The Bonze, Trouble

Mimi, Rodolfo, Marcello, Colline, Alcindoro, Parpignol, Musetta

Carmen, Don José, Escamillo, Zuniga, Frasquita, Mercedes

Brünnhilde, Flosshilde, Grimhilde, Siegfried

Amahl, Kaspar, Melchior, Balthasar

Figaro, Rosina, Almaviva, Fiorello, Basilio, Bartolo

Aïda, Radames, Amneris, Ramphis, Amonasro
Mephistopheles, Mephisto
Pelleas and Melisande
Dido, Aeneas, Belinda
Hansel and Gretel
Capriccio
Minnie, Dick, Billy Jackrabbit, Wowkle
Lohengrin, Ortrud, Elsa
Orpheus and Euridyce
Truelove, Tom Rakewell, Nick Shadow, Mother Goose, Baba the Turk
Rigoletto, Gilda, Sparafucile
Tristan and Isolde
Porgy, Bess, Sporting Life, Crown, Serena
Samson and Delilah
Tosca, Cavaradossi, Scarpia, Angelotti, Spoletta
Salome and Jokanaan
Violetta and Alfredo
Parsifal, Amfortas

Gilbert and Sullivan

Gilbert and Sullivan operettas are full of colorful characters with colorful names quite suitable for colorful cats. Obviously, the names Gilbert and Sullivan would be fine for a couple of cats, and for a litter of kittens, Nanki-Poo, Yum-Yum, Ko-Ko, Pooh-Bah, Pish-Tish, Pitti-Sing, Peep-Bo and Katisha.

Little Buttercup
Marmaduke Pointdextre
John Wellington Wells
Lady Sangazure
Ralph Rackstraw
Dick Deadeye
Bill Bobstay
Tom Tucker
Reginald Bunthorne
Lady Jane
Major General Stanley
Mabel
Frederic

Iolanthe
Private Willis
Princess Ida
Hilarion
Melissa
Sacharissa
Robin Oakapple
Richard Dauntless
Sir Despard Murgatroyd
Adam Goodheart
Rose Maybud
Mad Margaret
Dame Hannah

Great Composers

For serious, weighty cats:

Johannes Brahms
Johann Sebastian Bach
Ludwig van Beethoven
Wolfgang Amadeus Mozart
Felix Mendelssohn
George Frideric Handel
Henry Purcell
Antonio Vivaldi
Arcangelo Corelli

Domenico Scarlatti
Frederic Chopin
Claude Debussy
Maurice Ravel
Georges Bizet
Modest Mussorgsky
Igor Stravinsky
Peter Ilyich Tchaikovsky

Contemporary Music

Jimmie Rodgers
Red Sovine
Merle Haggard
Johnny Cash
Alvin Crow
Tammy Wynette
Loretta Lynn
Dolly Parton
Waylon, Willie and Kenny
Kristofferson
Elvis
John, Paul, George and Ringo
Yoko Ono
Simon and Garfunkel
Peter, Paul and Mary
Pete Seeger
Dylan
Arlo
Joan Baez
Sonny and Cher
Mick Jagger
Jimi Hendrix
Crosby, Stills and Nash

Blondie
Billy Joel
Liberty deVito
Fleetwood Mac
Elton John
Reo Speedwagon
Jellyroll Morton
Howlin Wolf
Cab Calloway
Washboard Sam
Muddy Waters
Ethel Waters
Mahalia
'Sippi
Sweet Peas
Alberta Hunter
Ella
Aretha
Diana
Otis Redding
Ray Charles
Little Richard
Wicked Wilson Pickett

Musicals

Ziegfeld
Rodgers and Hammerstein

Artful Dodger
Anna and the King of Siam

Oklahoma

Annie Oakley

Judd

South Pacific

Camelot

Liza Doolittle

Alfred Doolittle

Henry Higgins

Gypsy

Mama Rose

Mr. Goldstone

Oliver

Fagin

Bill Sykes

Candide

Dr. Pangloss

Hair

Dancin'

Annie

Daddy Warbucks

Sweeney Todd

No No Nanette

Dolly

Phineas T. Barnum

Evita

Sugar Baby

Tommy Tune

Twiggy

ART

Botticelli
Cimabue
Giotto
Giorgione
Leonardo
Michelangelo
Modigliani
Raphael
Sassetta
Tintoretto
Titian
Uccello
Veronese
Verrocchio
Cézanne
Degas
Fragonard
Gauguin
Magritte
Matisse
Renoir
Rousseau
Toulouse-Lautrec
Utrillo
Vigée-Lebrun
El Greco
Goya
Murillo
Picasso

Velásquez
Cranach
Holbein
Rembrandt
Van Gogh
Van Dyke
Vermeer
Constable
Gainsborough
Hogarth
Landseer
Raeburn
Romney
Stubbs
Turner
Cassatt
de Kooning
Frankenthaler
Gorky
Olitski
Oldenburg
Pollock
Nevelson
Rauschenberg
Sargent
Stella
Warhol
Whistler
Zox

Shakespeare

A young man who owned a game parlor, where vicious games of chess and backgammon were played and Russian grandmasters occasionally showed up, got himself a dog and two cats and called them Hamlet, Rosencrantz and Guildenstern, in that order. When queried by his mother about his choice of names, all he would reveal, darkly, was that he liked a connecting thread. However, not too long thereafter, he sold his business and enrolled in the Stella Adler Studio to study method acting and now is never seen without a brooding expression on his face and a copy of *Hamlet* sticking out of his back pocket.

Shakespeare is full of good names for cats.

Hamlet, Horatio, Gertrude, Polonius, Ophelia, Rosencrantz and Guildenstern, Fortinbras

Macbeth, Macduff, Lady Macbeth (whose first name was Gruoch)

Othello, Desdemona, Iago

Oberon, Titania, Puck, Robin Goodfellow, Peaseblossom, Cobweb, Moth, Mustardseed

Romeo and Juliet

Antony and Cleopatra

Lysander, Demetrius, Hippolyte, Hermia, Quince, Snug, Bottom, Flute, Starveling

Falstaff, Mistress Quickly, Doll Tearsheet, Bardolph, Pistol, Shallow, Silence, Fang, Snake

Prospero, Ariel, Miranda, Caliban

Florizel, Perdita, Mopsa, Dorcas

Mistress Overdone

Pinch

Touchstone

Montjoy

Dogberry

Simple

Rugby

Elbow

Froth

Other good names from the theater

Aeschylus

Sophocles

Euripides

Aristophanes

Ariosto

Kabuki

Richard Burbage

Faustus

Mother Bombie

Tartuffe

Colley Cibber

Goldoni

Garrick

Mrs. Siddons

Minna von Barnhelm

Edwin Booth

Sarah Bernhardt

Duse

Mrs. Patrick Campbell

Ellen Terry

Lily Langtry

Lillian Russell

Hedda Gabler

Nora

Major Barbara

Pygmalion

Ethel, John and Lionel

Pirandello

Belasco

Tallulah

Sybil Thorndyke

Zero

Harvey

Blanche du Bois

Stanley and Stella

Sebastian and Violet

Summer and Smoke

Willie Loman

Mousetrap

Godot

Ondine

Hume and Jessica

Auntie Mame

Miss Jean Brodie

Marat and Sade

Blue Morphan

True West

DANCE

Eglevsky
Fokine
Petipa
Grisi
Taglioni
Ceccheti
Nijinski
Nijinska
Diaghilev
Pavlova
Fonteyn
Moira Shearer
Nureyev
Baryshnikov
Maria Tallchief
Pina Bausch
Malusardi
Entrechat
Pas de Chat
Jeté
Isadora

Miss de Mille
Martha Graham
Merce
Béjart
Valda Setterfield
Strathspey
Jig
Hornpipe
Fandango
Squaredance
Charleston
Twist
Softshoe
Ginger Rogers
Fred Astaire
Busby Berkley
Bojangles
Ruby Keeler
Little Egypt
Gypsy Rose Lee

LITERATURE

Melville
Mark Twain
Henry James
Scott and Zelda
Papa Hemingway
Gertrude Stein
Alice B. Toklas
B. Traven
Hammett and Hellman
Mickey Spillane
Anaïs Nin
Eudora
Willa
Mary McCarthy
Sam Pepys
Dickens
Thackeray
Charlotte and Emily
Virginia Woolf
Bloomsbury
D.H.
Isherwood
Agatha
Du Maurier
Stendhal
Zola
Marcel Proust
Amandine Aurore Lucie Dupin
Colette
Sagan
Dostoevsky
Tolstoy
Chekhov
Pasternak
Kafka
Boccaccio
Huckleberry
Fanny
Papa Daddy
Stella Rondo

Portnoy
Studs Lonigan
Balthazar B.
Myra Breckenridge
Désirée
Gatsby and Daisy
Lady Brett
Jake Barnes
Sartoris
Snopes
Temple Drake
Joe Christmas
Franny and Zooey
Seymour Glass
Holden Caulfield
Lolita
Augie March
Herzog
Mr. Sammler
Moll Flanders
Tom Jones
Heathcliff and Catherine
Mr. Rochester
Jane Eyre
Jeanie Dean
Lorna Doone
Rebecca
George Fortesquieu Maximilian de Winter
Mrs. Danvers
Gully Jimson
Jeeves
Bertie Wooster
Zuleika Dobson
Raskolnikov
Count Vronsky
Anna Karenina
Dr. Zhivago
Lara

PHILOSOPHY

Lao-tse
Pythagoras
Confucius
Empedocles
Socrates
Democritus
Plato
Aristotle
Epicurus
Zeno
Titus
Al-Farabi
Chu Hsi
Thomas Aquinas
Albertus Magnus
Savonarola
Descartes
Pascal
Spinoza
Leibnitz

Vico
Montesquieu
Voltaire
Hume
Diderot
Helvétius
Immanuel Kant
Rousseau
Hegel
Schopenhauer
Ralph Waldo Emerson
Thoreau
Kierkegaard
Nietzsche
Poincaré
Bergson
Heidegger
Rabindranath Tagore
Husserl
Wittgenstein

HISTORY

Hammurabi
Mark Antony
Marco Polo
Galileo
Henry Morgan
John Paul Jones
Metternich
Peter Porter
Paul Revere
Tippoo Sahib
George and Martha
Ben Franklin
Tom Jefferson
Danton
Robespierre
Charlotte Corday
Talleyrand
Horatio Nelson
Emma Hamilton
Garibaldi
Bismarck
Florence Nightingale
Beau Brummel
Von Clausewitz
Dr. Livingstone
Mr. Stanley
Mr. Gladstone
Mr. Disraeli
Santa Anna
Davy Crockett
Johnny Appleseed
Custer
Sam Colt
Charles Chubb
Harriet Beecher Stowe
J. P. Morgan
Rockefeller
Carnegie
Henry Ford
Grace Darling

Charles Stewart Parnell
Kitty O'Shea
Bernardo O'Higgins
Oliver Wendell Holmes
Amelia Bloomer
Jenny Lind
Mrs. Beeton
Lord Kitchener
Commodore Perry
Admiral Farragut
Ulysses S. Grant
Robert E. Lee
Lloyd George
Harold Harmsworth
Madame Curie
Octavia Hill
Rosa Luxemburg
Mrs. Pankhurst
Alexander Graham Bell
George Cadbury
Karl Marx
Lenin
Trotsky
Sun Yat-sen
Albert Schweitzer
Margaret Sanger
Samuel Gompers
Eugene Debs
H. L. Mencken
Clarence Darrow
Sacco
Vanzetti
Lizzie Borden
Amelia Earhart
Lucky Lindbergh
Evangeline Booth
Sigmund Freud
Carl Jung
Jonas Salk

MODERN TIMES

On the occasion of her thirtieth birthday, a friend decided
to throw a party to console herself. Remembering my own,
I went along, glad to offer my support, and spent the first
half of the evening talking to her cats Magritte and Cassatt
(she had majored in art history) and the second half talking
to a handsome young Princetonian. We got on like a house
on fire, seated on the floor, drinking wine and talking wit-
tily and at length about Robert Caro's biography of Lyndon
Johnson. His last, blithe remark as we parted was, "Of course,
Lyndon was a bit before my time." This left me speechless,
ruefully reflecting on the days when a Princeton man was
the last gasp in quite a different way. Notwithstanding, for
the purposes of this text, Modern Times begin somewhere
around the end of World War II.

America First
World War II
D-Day
Yalta
Franklin and Eleanor
Winston and Clemmy
Rommel and Monty
Charles de Gaulle
Patton
MacArthur
Ike and Mamie
JFK and Jacqueline
Bobby and Ethel
Teddy and Joan
Lyndon and Ladybird
Martin and Coretta
Jesse Jackson
Malcolm X
Huey P. Newton
Rap Brown
Stokley and Miriam
Eldridge and Kathy
Angela Y. Davis
Flower Power

Haight-Ashbury
Woodstock
Maryjane
Chairman Mao
Chou En-lai
Ho Chi Minh
Madame Nu
Christine Keeler
Fidel
Che Guevara
Huelga
Cesar Chavez
Muhammad Ali
Milhous
Kissinger
Jaworsky
Watergate
Woodward and Bernstein
Frank Lloyd Wright
Bella Abzug
Nancy Hanks
Letty Cottin Pogrebin
Gloria Steinem
Ayatollah

I deliberately omitted from the preceding list the names of people I considered too depraved to name a cat after. However, just before we went to press I went to a party in a palatial townhouse off Riverside Drive where I met a Jewish lady of evident culture and sensitivity. Some years ago this lady owned a white cat with a black moustache, who bore a startling resemblance to Adolf Hitler. Whenever she took her cat out, people would stop her and say, "My God, your cat looks just like Adolf Hitler." So what else could she call it? Let your conscience be your guide.

THE MYSTIC AND THE OCCULT

Isis
Bastet
Hecate
Zarathustra
Ormuzd
Nostradamus
Paracelsus
Meister Eckhart
Swedenborg
Ramakrishna
Vivekananda
Madame Blavatsky
Annie Besant
Krishnamurti
Gurdjieff
Alice Bailey

Talbot Mundy
Lobsang Rampa
Aimée Semple McPherson
Edgar Cayce
Arthur Ford
Kreskin
Silver Belle
Madame Flora
Ethel Post Parrish
Viola Osgood Dunne
Seth
Karma
Ouija
Trumpet
Apport

GEMS

Diamond
Ruby
Emerald
Topaz
Amethyst
Aquamarine
Garnet
Tourmaline
Zircon

Opal
Turquoise
Moonstone
Jade
Pearl
Amber
Coral
Jet

I was once lured to a small Presbyterian college within the boundaries of the Navaho reservation in northern Arizona by the promise of meeting the legendary Rosabelle Furcap; but by the time I got there she had long gone to Tuba City and I never did taste the Navaho tacos and fried bread for which she was famous. I have learned, and forgotten, and learned again, that when something is taken away, by some cosmic law of recompense something is given in its place.

My gift was Amy, a little Anglo girl of six who could speak Navaho with her friends when she didn't want her mother to know their plans. A few weeks before, her dog had had ten puppies whom Amy had named with dispatch—Strawberry Shortcake, Rosie, Teddy Bear, Max, Silver, Nosey, Sawdust, Coldy, Buttons and Potsie—and for which her equally resourceful mother had already found promised homes.

Amy was given a kitten by a professor of English who had twenty-five cats. The kitten resented being taken away from her mother and her special playmate, whose name was Pretty Boy. To communicate her distress she set up an endless, high-pitched, piercing whine very much like a whistling teakettle. Amy immediately named her Teapot, the lateral move being easy for a fan of Garfield. Teapot was adamant about being reunited with her loved ones and was eventually returned to the professor's household, which looks rather like a George Booth cartoon, where she romps happily with one and all.

Other cats Amy has named are: Snowflake (white), Blueberry (blue), Pizza (red), Orange and Lemon (yellow), Midnight (black), Hazy Day and Rain (gray), Raspberry (calico), Squirrel (bushy tail) and Exxon (found at a gas station). The Gift, like the Force, runs strong in some families.

Then, one evening as I leaned over a garden gate on the outskirts of the campus, the pink feathers of the tamarisk trees blown gently against my cheek by the spring wind, four young braves rode out of the Navaho dusk. They were lithe and lean and handsome, each traditionally dressed with a narrow red bandana around his forehead, shirt belted over his trousers, a silver buckle gleaming at his waist. They rode by silently, for their horses were unshod, looking neither to the right nor to the left, and the sight of them seared my soul and silenced rowdy Wags, the little dog at my feet.

So might they have ridden by in the days when they were called the lords of the earth, though I might have been less sanguine.

Barboncito	Black Kettle
Manuelito	Black Elk
Delgadito	Black Hawk
Largo	Red Cloud
Herrero	Red Jacket
Armijo	Red Sleeves
Torivio	Redbird
Ganado Mucho	Kicking Bird
Sitting Bull	Little Crow
Crazy Horse	Little Raven
Chief Joseph	Little Wolf
Chief Seattle	Lone Wolf
Luther Standing Bear	Spotted Tail
Chief Cornplant	Dull Knife
Chief Plenty Coups	Medicine Bottle
Tecumseh	Looking Glass
Big Bear	Hiawatha
Lean Bear	Minnehaha
Kicking Bear	Nokomis
Chased by Bears	Powhatan
Black Bear	Pocahontas

Borrow a Name

It may well be that your interests are narrow and your cat still unnamed. Don't give up hope, there are more ways than one to name a cat.

One aspect of the art of living is to know a good thing when you see it, to borrow it and to put it to good use at the first opportunity. A name can be swiped.

My childhood sweetheart, whom I left on the bonnie banks of Loch Lomond, where he is to this day, had an uncle who in his youth used to sail around the Caribbean in wintertime to keep warm. One day this uncle set foot on a small island, uninhabited except for a tiny settlement of people of African descent, where he was introduced to a little dog named Raindrop. Fresh water being scarce on the island and rain much prayed for, it was clear that the dog was precious to his owner. The uncle set sail again, acquired a little dog, and being a canny Scot, called it Raindrop. It was the first of a long line of Raindrops in his life. His sister, mother of my friend, was also smitten with the name. Not to be outdone, she herself got a little dog, called it Raindrop, passed the name down through several generations of little dogs, and still has a Raindrop to this day. Rarely have I encountered a name put to better or more assiduous use, and the first kitten I found after hearing this story I named Raindrop.

So cast around in your childhood memories, inquire

among your friends or borrow the name of a well-known cat.

Another name I borrowed was that of Thomasina, the orange cat in the movie *The Three Lives of Thomasina,* based on the novel by Paul Gallico. In the movie is a scene in which the cat sits out on the branch of a tree, soaked to the skin in a Scottish downpour, refusing his young mistress's pleas to come indoors—a scene through which I wept piteously. Now, in my first alley was an orange cat, an older daughter of Mother Cat, who had never really left home or had kittens of her own. Like her mother she was wild (I still have the scar to prove it). Sometimes on rainy days I would see her huddle in a doorway. My heart went out to her; up flew my kitchen window and a well-aimed beef kidney would land at her toes. What they lacked in lodgings, Thomasina and her mother made up for in food. The men who worked in a nearby fish market tossed them a dozen jumbo shrimp every day but Sunday, and an occasional can of crabmeat.

Other famous names you might borrow are:

Mehitabel from the Archy and Mehitabel stories by Don Marquis

Muezza, the cat who belonged to the prophet Mohammed, for whom he had such tender regard that he cut off the hem of his cloak rather than disturb her sleep

Macavity, Mungojerrie and Old Deuteronomy, the most famous of T. S. Eliot's practical cats

Figaro, who belonged to Pinocchio, then got himself on a cat food can

Atossa, from the poem *Mathias and Atossa* by Matthew Arnold

Selima, of the *Ode on the Death of a Favourite Cat, Drowned in a Tub of Gold Fishes,* by Thomas Gray

Hodge, the cat belonging to Samuel Johnson, who always went out to buy oysters for it lest his housekeeper take a dislike to the cat from having to do so

Fletcher, from the story *Fletcher and Zenobia*

Tobermory, the talking cat in a story by Saki

Ivan, from *Peter and the Wolf*

Hamlet, who lives in the lobby of the Hotel Algonquin

Morris, who sells Nine Lives cat food on television

Rhubarb, who was a star of film and television before I set foot in this country

Felix the Cat from the comic strip of the same name
Krazy Kat from the comic strip by George Herriman
Sylvester from the series of animated films costarring Sweetie
  Pie
Tom from the Tom and Jerry series of animated films

The Tibetan Way

One thing I've come to realize is that the questions I ask about *life* are really questions about myself at a particular juncture of my life. Sometimes I need help in rephrasing them in order to be clear about what I'm really asking. Then invariably I have found the answers are within me and all I need is a way to bring them forth. There are many ways to go about this, most of which call for relaxation and meditation. I asked a friend, more spiritually advanced than myself, to work out a method of meditation that will help bring forth your cat's name. So if it is still eluding you, you might do well to try the following.

Relax yourself by lying on your back on the floor with your knees raised and your feet firmly on the ground. Breathe gently and regularly, concentrating on the exhale, and try to clear your mind of clutter. This is sometimes easier said than done, and it helps if you acknowledge the distractions in your mind, rather than just trying to push them down. Let them rise to the surface and float away. If you are new to meditation and these distractions continue to bother you, repeat the following mantra silently to the rhythm of your breathing. *Ham/Sah*. *Ham* on the inhale and *Sah* on the exhale.

Ten minutes of this is probably as much as you will be able to do in the beginning. Repeat the exercise every day until your mind begins to feel clear and empty. It doesn't matter

how long it takes for you to accomplish this, time is of no concern. When you feel ready, proceed to the next step.

Certain Tibetan mystics who want to attain the qualities of a particular Tibetan deity first study the god's image very intently and in the minutest detail. Then they close their eyes and try to reproduce the image of the god in all its complexity inside themselves. If you've ever seen a Tibetan deity you'll realize that this is no mean feat. A cat is easy by comparison. My friend recommends that you look closely, intently and lovingly at your cat, observing every little whisker and eyelash and the details of his markings. Then, having relaxed yourself and cleared your mind as much as possible, close your eyes and try to visualize your cat in perfect detail. Sooner or later the essence of your cat's personality will reveal itself to you, and a name will rise from the depths of your subconscious to fit it, and that will be the best possible name you could have chosen for your cat.

Do not upbraid yourself over spiritual shortcomings if this method does not work for you. It will not advance you along the Path one jot if you do. Anyhow, where you are spiritually is nobody's business but your own. It may well be that you have sat there, your cat by your side, and read assiduously through this book, trying this and discarding that, and your cat is still nameless. Do not be discouraged. Turn but a few more pages and you will find over 4000 names for your cat. You will have come across many of them in the preceding pages, but there are plenty of fresh ones to choose from and surely you will find one that suits your cat.

Do Our Cats Name Us?

Human names cat. But how about the obverse? Do our cats also name us? And what in cat do they call us if they do? A batch of my nephews raised for the most part in the north of Yorkshire were overheard referring to their disciplinary Scottish grandmother as the old haggis. Over the years, I've often had the suspicion that my own cats and the disadvantaged felines I've sheltered have had a similar name for me.

No, you cannot pee on my grapefruit tree, Desdemona! *Yeeeooouuw!* (Spoilsport?)

Dammit, Ashley, do you have to throw up on my only cashmere sweater!? *Yeerreeaaa!* (Bitch?)

Agamemnon, if you beat up Billy one more time, it's back to the waterfront where I found you! *Yaaarrraaagh!* (M———r?)

Of epithets I'm almost certain. That they communicate their needs and wants, their pleasure and displeasure, there is no doubt. A cat wakes up in another room and miaows plaintively that he's alone in the world. I hasten to reassure him that we are all nearby and won't he please come and join us. He's of a skeptical nature and asks how can he be sure that my voice is not an illusion? So I walk to the door of the other room and say, "Here I am, and I've saved you some cream from my strawberries." Soon he's purring happily and telling me how glad he is I took him in off the streets.

Perhaps intermingled in this conversation is his name for me, which I respond to unknowingly. My former husband swore that Humphrey and Dolly and Bean Blossom called me the Big Hamburger and perhaps he wasn't far wrong. A cat's love and loyalty are very closely connected to the dishing out of food. Perhaps their names for us are variations of O Thou Who Feeds Me. But until we crack the code we'll never know for sure.

Maybe someday in the long course of evolution, cats will invite humans into their homes and we'll go gladly and quickly, learn our names and make the grateful, friendly sounds that insure us food, shelter and love. Until that time the honor of naming the cat is ours and as long as we're in the catbird seat, we might as well enjoy ourselves.

Cats from A to Z
Over 4000 Cat Names

Abelard
Aberdeen
Abigail
Acapulco
Ace
Achernar
Achilles
Ackroyd
Adam Goodheart
Addis Ababa
Addison
Adelaide
Admiral Farragut
Adolf
Aeneas
Aeschylus
Africa
Agamemnon
Agatha
Agnes
Agronsky
Aïda
Aimée Semple McPherson
Ainsley
Ajax
Akasaka
Akbar the Great
Al Capone
Al-Farabi
Alabama

Alamo
Alan Ladd
Albert
Albert Schweitzer
Albert the Bear
Alberta Hunter
Albertus Magnus
Albuquerque
Alcindoro
Aldebaran
Alekhine
Alexander
Alexander Graham Bell
Alexander the Great
Alexandra
Alfa Romeo
Alfalfa
Alfonso the Wise
Alfred
Alfred Doolittle
Alfred the Great
Alfred, Lord Tennyson
Algonquin
Ali Baba
Alice
Alice B. Toklas
Alice Bailey
Alimony
Alka-Seltzer
Allecto

Allegra
Almaviva
Almond
Alonso
Aloysius
Alpha Centauri
Alpha Crucis
Alphonse
Altair
Althea
Alvin Crow
Amadeus
Amagansett
Amahl
Amanda
Amandine Aurore Lucie Dupin
Amarillo
Amaryllis
Amber
Ambrose
Amelia Bloomer
Amelia Earhart
America First
Amerigo
Amethyst
Amfortas
Aminhotep
Amneris
Amonasro
Amphora
Anaïs Nin
Anastasia
Andorra
Andrea Doria
Andrew
Andrew Aguecheek
Andromeda
Anemone
Angel
Angela Y. Davis
Angelica
Angelo
Angelotti
Angus
Anna & the King of Siam
Anna Karenina
Anna Moffo
Annabelle
Anne Boleyn
Annie

Annie Besant
Annie Hall
Annie Oakley
Annunciata
Anonymous
Anselmo
Antares
Antony
Anthracite
Antigone
Antoine
Antonia
Antonio
Antonid
Apollo
Apple
Appleblossom
Appleby
Applepie
Appolonius
Apport
Aquamarine
Aquila
Arabella
Archangel
Arcturus
Aretha
Ariadne
Ariel
Aries
Ariosto
Aristophanes
Aristotle
Arizona
Arkansas
Arlo
Armand
Arna Bontemps
Artemidorus
Artemis
Artful Dodger
Arthur Ashe
Arthur Ford
Artichoke
Artis
Arugula
Arvid
Ash Wednesday
Ashbery
Ashby

Ashes
Ashkenazy
Ashley Wilkes
Asia
Asparagus
Atalanta
Athabasca
Athena
Atlanta
Atossa
Attila the Hun
Audrey
Augie March
Augusta
Augustus
Auntie Mame
Aurelia
Auriga
Aurora
Austin
Axle
Ayatollah
Aylesworthy
Azalea

Baba the Turk
Babe Ruth
Babushka
Baby
Baby Doe
Baby Jane
Babyboots
Baby's-Breath
Bacall
Bach
Backfire
Baghdad
Bailey
Bakersfield
Balderdash
Balfour
Balthasar
Balthazar B.
Banana
Bandit
Banjo
Bannister
Barbara Walters
Barbarella
Barbarosa

Barboncito
Barcelona
Bardolph
Barley
Barnaby
Barnacle
Barabbas
Bars
Bartleby
Bartholomew
Bartlett
Bartolo
Baryshnikov
Basil
Basilio
Bastet
Bathsheba
Batman
Bean Blossom
Beansprout
Bear
Beasley
Beatrix
Beau
Beau Brummel
Beaulieu
Beauregard
Beautiful
Bebe
Beekman
Beelzebub
Beena
Beeswax
Beethoven
Beetroot
Béjart
Belafonte
Belasco
Belerophon
Belinda
Bella Abzug
Belle Starr
Belmont
Belushi
Ben
Benedict
Ben Franklin
Bengal
Benjamin
Benjamino

Bennington
Benoni
Bentley
Beowulf
Beresford
Bergson
Berlin
Bernardo O'Higgins
Bernice
Bernstein
Bert
Bertha
Bertie Wooster
Bertram
Bess
Beta Centauri
Beta Crucis
Betelgeuse
Bethesda
Beverly
Bianca
Biff
Big
Big Bear
Bijou
Billingsgate
Bill Bailey
Bill Bobstay
Bill Sykes
Billie Jean
Billy Budd
Billy J. Smith
Billy Jackrabbit
Billy Joel
Bimbo
Bird Bones
Birgit Nilsson
Biscuit
Bismarck
Bittersweet
Bituminous
Bizet
Bjorn Borg
Black Bear
Black Elk
Black Hawk
Black Kettle
Blackberry
Blackie
Blackjack

Blacklegs
Blake
Blanc Mange
Blanche
Blanche Du Bois
Blimpie
Blondie
Bloomsbury
Blotter
Blue
Blue Eyes
Blue Morphan
Bluebell
Blueberry
Bluebird
Bluebottle
Bo-Peep
Bob
Bobby Fischer
Bobby Wombles
Boccaccio
Bogart
Bogie
Bogolyubov
Bojangles
Boleslavski
Bombay
Bonanza
Bonaparte
Boney
Bonita
Bonnie
Bonnie Dundee
Bonnie Parker
Bonnie Prince Charlie
the Bonze
Bootsie
Borgov
Boris
Bosco
Bossy
Boston
Boswell
Botticelli
Bottom
Bounty
Bradley
Brahms
Bramble
Brandenburg

91

Brandy
Breakspear
Breathless
Breeches
Brendan
Bridget
Brigitte Bardot
Brillo
Brimstone
Brinkley
Brinley
Broadway
Broderick Crawford
Brooke
Brooklyn
Broom Hilda
Browning
Brünnhilde
B. Traven
Bubble and Squeak
Bubbles
Bucephalus
Buck Rogers
Buckeye
Buckminster
Budapest
Bugatti
Bugsy Siegel
Bull Run
Bumblebee
Bunny
Bunsen
Burberry
Burns
Burton
Bus Moran
Bus Stop
Busby Berkley
Bushy
Buster Brown
Busybody
Butch Cassidy
Buttercup
Butterscotch
Butterwort
Buttons
Byron

Cabbage
Cab Calloway

Cadbury
Caesar
Caitlin
Caldonia
Caliban
Caligula
Caliope
Caliopsis
Calypso
Camelia
Camelot
Cameron
Camille
Camillo Pabis Ticci
Campbell's Soup
Canapus
Candide
Canute
Capablanca
Capella
Capriccio
Capricornus
Captain Bligh
Captain Bob
Captain Hook
Capulet
Cara
Caracas
Carburetor
Carissima
Carl Jung
Carlotta
Carlton
Carmel
Carmen
Carmichael
Carnegie
Carolina
Caroline
Carruthers
Casaba
Casablanca
Casamassima
Cashew
Casimir
Casper
Cassandra
Cassatt
Cassiopeia
Cassius

Cat o'War
Catesby
Catharine the Great
Cathead
Catnip Herb
Catsby
Cauliflower
Cavaradossi
Ceccheti
Cecil
Cecil Cooper
Cecilia
Celeste
Cesar Chavez
Cesare
Cézanne
Chairman Mao
Chambliss
Chameleon
Champagne
Chang Wo
Charcoal
Charisse
Charity
Charlemagne
Charles
Charles and Diana
Charles de Gaulle
Charles Stewart Parnell
Charles the Bold
Charles the Fat
Charles the Good
Charles the Simple
Charleston
Charlie
Charlotte
Charlotte Corday
Charlton
Chased by Bears
Chattanooga
Chaucer
Chauncey
Che Guevara
Checkmate
Chekhov
Chelsea
Cheops
Chervil
Chester
Chevy

Chewbacca
Cheyenne
Chicken Noodle
Chickpea
Chico and The Man
Chief Cornplant
Chief Joseph
Chief Plenty Coups
Chief Seattle
China
Chintsel
Chip Glass
Chippewa
Chivers
Chloe
Choke
Cholmondley
Chopin
Chopsticks
Chou En-lai
Christian
Christianna
Christie
Christina Rossetti
Christine Keeler
Christmas
Christopher
Christopher Reeve
Chrysanthemum
Chu Hsi
Chubb
Chuckles
Churchill
Cicero
Cicero Murphy
Cimabue
Cimarron
Cincinnati
Cinderella
Cinders
Cinnamon
Cio-Cio San
Circe
Cissy
Citrus
Clancy
Clarence
Clarence Darrow
Claude
Claudell Washington

Claudia
Claudius
Clematis
Clemence
Clementina
Clemmy
Cleopatra
Cleveland
Clove
Clover
Clyde
Clyde Barrow
Clytemnestra
Coal Dust
Cobweb
Cochineal
Cochise
Cocoa
Coconut
Coffin
Coke
Colby
Cole
Coleen
Colette
Colley Cibber
Colorado
Columbia
Columbine
Commodore Perry
Concepción
Confucius
Constable
Constance
Consuelo
Cookie Lavagetto
Cooper
Copycat
Cora
Coral
Cordelia
Corelli
Coretta
Corky
Cornbread
Cornelia Meigs
Cornelius
Cornell Macneil
Cosimo
Cotton

Cottontail
Coughdrop
Count Vronsky
Countee Cullen
Crabapple
Crackerbarrel
Cranach
Crankshaft
Crawdaddy
Crawford
Crazy Horse
Cricket
Crisco
Cromwell
Cronkite
Crosby
Crosby, Stills and Nash
Crossfire
Crosspatch
Crowflower
Crown
Crumpet
Crystal
C3PO
Cuckoo
Cuckoo-Bud
Cuddles
Culloden
Culpepper
Cumberland
Cumin
Cunegonde
Cupid
Curiosity
Custard
Custer
Cutter
Cygnus
Cynthia
Czarina

Dab
Dabble
Daddy Warbucks
Daffodil
Dagwood
Dahlia
Daimler
Daiquiri
Daisy

Dakota
Dalhousie
Dallas
Damascus
Damocles
Damon
Damosel
Damson
Danbury.
Dancin'
Dandelion
Dandy
Danegeld
Daniel
Dante
Dante Lavelli
Danton
Danvers
Danzig
Daphne
Dapple
D'Arcy
Darius
Darjeeling
Darkling
Darkstar
Darling
Darrell Porter
Darth Vader
Dartmouth
Darwin
Dash
Daumier
Dauntless
Dauphin
Davenport
Davis
Davy Crockett
Dawdle
Dawn
Dazzler
D-Day
de Kooning
de Witt
Deadeye
Deadlock
Dean the Dream
Deauville
Debussy
Defiance

Degas
Deirdre
Delaware
Delilah
Deliverance
Delmonte
Delmore
Delphinus
Demetrius
Demitasse
Democritus
Denver
De Quincey
Derby
Derry
Descartes
Desdemona
Désirée
Desmond
Detroit
Detroit Whitey
Deuce
Deuteronomy
Dewdrop
D.H.
Diaghilev
Diamond
Diamond Lil
Diana
Dick
Dickens
Diderot
Dido
Diego
Diesel
Dietrich
Digby
Dill
Dillinger
Dillon
Dillweed
Dim Sum
Dimbleby
Dimitri
Dimples
Dinah
Diplodicus
Dips-A-Little
Dipstick
Disco

95

Dish
Disraeli
Diva
Divine
Divisadero
Dixie
Dixon
Dizzy
Djakarta
Dobson
Dockage
Doctor Dunk
Doctor J
Doctor Snuggles
Dodge
Dofu
Dogbane
Dogberry
Dogood
Dogwood
Dolabella
Dolly
Dolly Parton
Dolores
Dombrowsky
Domino
Donahue
Donatello
Donegal
Donnybrook
Doorstop
Doppelgänger
Dora
Dorcas
Doris
Dorothy
Dory
Dostoevsky
Doubting Thomas
Douglas
Downhill
Dr. Jeckyll
Dr. Livingstone
Dr. No
Dr. Pangloss
Dr. Zhivago
Dragonfly
Dream
Driftwood
Drusilla

Du Maurier
Dubarry
Dublin
Duchamp
Dudgeon
Dudley
Dufy
Dulciana
Dulcie
Dull Knife
Dumas
Dumpling
Dunbar
Dundee
Dundreary
Dunfermline
Dungaree
Dunsmore
Dunwoodie
Durango
Duse
Düsseldorf
Dustin
Dusty
Dutch Schultz
Dylan
Dynamo
Dynasty

Eager
Eagle
Eaglesham
Eakins
Eames
Eamonn
Earhart
Earl
Earl the Pearl
Early
Earnshaw
Earth
Eartha
Earthbound
Earthstar
Eastend
Easter
Eastman Kodak
Eastside
Eastwind
Easy Street

Eatwell
Eavesdrop
Ebenezer
Ebenstein
Eboli
Ebony
Eccles
Echo
Edda
Edelweiss
Eden
Edgar
Edgar Allan Poe
Edgar Cayce
Edgar the Peaceful
Edgecombe
Edgewise
Edie
Edith
Edith Cavell
Edmond
Edna
Edna St. Vincent Millay
Edsel
Eduardo
Edward
Edwin Booth
Edwina
Eggcream
Eggplant
Eggroll
Eggshell
Eggwhite
Eglantine
Eglevsky
Egypt
Eiderdown
Eiffel
Eight
Eightball
Einstein
El Cid
El Greco
El Morro
El Paso
El Toro
Elaine
Elastic
Elbow
Elbowgrease

Elderberry
Eldorado
Eldridge
Eleanor
Electra
Electric
Electrolux
Elegant
Elephant
Elf
Elgin
Elijah
Elixir
Eliza
Elizabeth
Elizabeth Barrett Browning
Elizabeth Regina
Elk
Ella
Ella Mae
Ellen Terry
Ellenbogen
Ellery
Elliot
Ellis Valentine
Ellsworth
Elm
Eloise
Elrod Hendricks
Elsa
Elsie Marley
Elsinore
Elton John
Elvis
Embassy
Ember
Embroidery
Emerald
Emergency
Emerson
Emigrant
Emily
Emily Dickinson
Emma Hamilton
Emmanuella
Emory
Empedocles
Empress
En Passant
Enchanted

Encore
Endgame
Endicott
Endive
Endless
Endymion
Enfant Terrible
England
Englebert
Enna Jettick
Enos Slaughter
Enrico Caruso
Entrechat
Entwhistle
Epicurus
Epiphany
Equanimity
Equus
Erasmus
Eric the Saint
Ermanno Mauro
Ermine
Ernestina
Ernesto
Escamillo
Escrow
Eskimo
Esmerelda
Estelle
E.T.
Ethel Post Parrish
Ethel Waters
Ethel, John and Lionel
Ethelred
Ethiopia
Eubanks
Euclid
Eudora
Eugene Debs
Eugenie
Eumenides
Euphemia
Euphon
Euphrates
Eureka
Euripides
Europa
Eurydice
Eustace
Eva

Evangeline Booth
Eve
Eveready
Evergreen
Everycat
Evian
Evinrude
Evita
Express
Exxon
Ezekiel
Ezra

Fabian
Fabulous
Fade In
Fagaras
Fagin
Fahrenheit
Fairbanks
Fairfield
Fairweather
Faisal
Faith
Faizabad
Fakir
Falcon
Falkbeer
Falkirk
Falkland
Fallacious
Falsetto
Falstaff
Famagusta
Fame
Fancy
Fandango
Fang
Fanny
Fanshaw
Faraway
Farina
Farrah Fawcett
Fast Eddie
Fatback
Fatcat
Fatima
Fatso
Faulkner
Faultless

Faustus
Faux Pas
Fawkes
Fawn
Feast
Feather
Fee Simple
Feedbag
Fegatello
Felicity
Felix
Fellow Traveller
Fenian
Fennel
Ferdinand
Fernando
Ferrari
Fetching
Fever
Fianchetto
Fiasco
Fickle
Fiddle
Fidel
Figaro
Filibuster
Fillmore
Finchley
Fingal
Finlay
Finsbury
Fiorello
Fireball
Firebrand
Firefly
Fireside
Firkin
Firstwater
Fish and Chips
Fisheye
Fishwife
Fitzcaraldo
Fitzgerald
Fitzgibbon
Fitzpatrick
Fitzsimmons
Fitzwater
Fitzwilliam
Five and Dime
Flagstone

Flako
Flamenco
Flamingo
Flanders
Flapper
Flash
Flattery
Flaubert
Fleet
Fleetwood Mac
Fletcher
Fleur
Flickers
Flinders
Flood
Flora
Florence
Florence Nightingale
Florizel
Flosshilde
Flotsam
Flounce
Flower Power
Flute
Fly by Night
Flyboy
Flywheel
Fnitten
Fog
Foghorn
Fokine
Fokker
Folderol
Folly
Folsom
Fomalhaut
Fonteyn
Fonz
Foolscap
Footloose
Footsteps
Ford
Forget-Me-Not
Fortinbras
Fortune
Foster
Fourflusher
Fox
Foxfire
Foxglove

Fraggle Rock
Fragonard
Francesca
Francis
Francis Bacon
Franco Corelli
François Villon
Frangipani
Frank Costello
Frank Lloyd Wright
Frankenstein
Frankenthaler
Frankie Frisch
Franklin
Franny
Franz Joseph
Frasquita
Frazzle
Fred
Fred Astaire
Frederica von Stade
Frederick
Frederick Barbarossa
Frederick the Great
Freeloader
Frenchie Faqua
Frenzy
Fresco
Freshwater
Friar
Frick
Friendless
Friendly
Frisbee
Frisky
Fritz
Frivolity
Frobisher
Frosh
Frost
Froth
Fu-cat-chu
Fuchsia
Fumble
Funny Face

Gable
Gadfly
Gadsden
Gainsborough

Gaiters
Gaitskell
Galahad
Gale
Galilee
Galileo
Gallant
Gallimaufry
Gallipoli
Galoshes
Galsworthy
Galveston
Galway
Ganado Mucho
Garbo
Gardez
Garibaldi
Garnet
Garozzo
Garrick
Garrison
Garter
Gaslight
Gatsby
Gauguin
Gazebo
Geary
Gem
Genesis
Geneva
Genghis Khat
Gentian
Geoffrey
Geordie
George Frideric Handel
George and Martha
George and Mary
George Fortesquieu Maximilian
    de Winter
Georgia
Georgie Girl
Georgina
Gepetto
Gerald
Geraldine
Gerlachovka
Geronimo
Gertrude
Gertrude Stein
Gibraltar

100

Gilbert
Gilda
Gillyvor
Gina
Ginger
Ginger Rogers
Gingerbread
Gingersnap
Ginsberg
Giorgio Belladonna
Giorgione
Giotto
Gladstone
Gladys
Glasgow
Glencora
Glengarry
Gloria
Gloria Steinem
Gloucester
Godfather
Godfrey
Godot
Godunov
Godwin
Goethe
Goggles
Goldfarb
Goldfinger
Goldoni
Goliath
Gompers
Goneril
Gonzalo
Goober
Good Morning, America
Good Queen Bess
Goody Two-Shoes
Googie
Goolagong
Gooseberry
Gorbuduc
Gorgeous Gussie
Gorilla
Gorky
Gospodin
Gossamer
Goulash
Goya
Grace Bumbry

Grace Darling
Gracie
Gradgrind
Graham
Gramercy
Grandslam
Granola
Grasshopper
Grassroots
Gray MacArthur
Graziana
Grease
Greeley
Greenhorn
Greer
Gregory
Grenadine
Grendel
Gresham
Gretchen
Griddle
Grimalkin
Grimhilde
Grimm
Grimsby
Gringo
Grisi
Grits
Grizzly
Grog
Groovie Goolies
Gropius
Groundhog
Grubstreet
Gruoch
Grudge
Guggenheim
Gullah
Gulliver
Gully Jimson
Gumbo
Gumdrop
Gumshoe
Gunshot
Gurdjieff
Guru
Gustavus Adolphus
Gusto
Guthrie
Gypsy

Gypsy Rose Lee

Haddington
Hades
Hadrian
Haggis
Haight-Ashbury
Hailey
Hair
Halloween
Hamburger
Hamlet
Hammett
Hammurabi
Han Solo
Handlebar
Hand-Me-Down
Hank Aaron
Hannibal
Hansel and Gretel
Harcourt
Hard Times
Hareball
Hargreaves
Harlan
Harlem
Harley Davidson
Harlow
Harmony
Harold
Harold Bluetooth
Harold Haarfagr
Harold Harmsworth
Harriet
Harriet Beecher Stowe
Harrison
Harrods
Harry
Hart Crane
Harun al-Rashid
Harvard
Harvey
Hastings
Hathaway
Hatteras
Haverford
Hawaiian Brian
Hawkeye
Haworth
Hawthorne

Haywire
Haze
Hazel
Hazy Day
Heathcliff
Heavy
Hecate
Heckle and Jeckle
Hedda Gabler
Heddy
Hedgehog
Hegel
Heidegger
Heigh Ho
Heinz
Helen
Hellbent
Hellman
Helmsley
Helvétius
Hemingway
Hemlock
Henri Quatre
Henry
Henry Ford
Henry Higgins
Henry James
Henry Morgan
Henry the Proud
Henry the Quarrelsome
Henry VIII
Hepburn
Herbie
Hercules
Herman
Herman the Ermine
Hermia
Hermione
Hero
Hershey
Herzog
Hesiod
Hester
Hetty
Hi Jack
Hi Jinks
Hiawatha
Hickory
Hidalgo
Higginson

Hilarion
Hilary
Hilda
Hilda Doolittle
Hildegard
Hill Street Blue
Hindsight
Hippolyte
Hirohito
Hirsute
Hispaniola
H. L. Mencken
Hoagie
Hoboken
Hobson
Ho Chi Minh
Hocuspocus
Hodge
Hofbauer
Hogan
Hogarth
Hogmanay
Hoi Polloi
Holbein
Holden Caulfield
Holly
Hollyhock
Homer
Honda
Hondo
Honey
Honeysuckle
Honora
Hood
Hoopla
Hopalong
Hopeful
Hopkins
Hopscotch
Hopsing
Horace
Horatio
Horatio Nelson
Hornet
Hornpipe
Horowitz
Hortense
Hot Lips Houlihan
Hotspur
Houston

Howard Duff
Howlin Wolf
Hubble
Hubcap
Hubie Brooks
Huckleberry
Huckster
Hudson
Huelga
Huey P. Newton
Huffy
Hugo
Humble
Humboldt
Hume
Humphrey
Hunky Dory
Hunter
Huntley and Brinkley
Hurricane
Husky
Hussar
Husserl
Hyacinth
Hydra

Iago
Ibadan
Ibiza
Ibo
Ibsen
Icarus
Icebox
Ice Cream
the Iceman
Ida Lupino
Idaho
Idlewild
Ignatius
Igor
Ike
Ilka
Illampu
Illinois
Illyria
Ilya Kuryakin
Imbroglio
Immanuel Kant
Imogene
IMP

Impatiens
Impossible
Impromptu
Imrez
In Memoriam
Inamorato
Inchmeal
Inchworm
Independence
India
Indiana Jones
Indigo
Indolent
Indoors
Indra
Indus
Inez
Ingersol
Inglewood
Ingram
Ingres
Ingrid
Iniquity
Inkberry
Inkster
Inky
Innocence
Innuendo
Insidious
Interlude
Inverness
Iolanthe
Iowa
Iphigenia
Iris
Irish
Irma
Ironblue
Ironsides
Ironweed
Irrawaddy
Irving
Isabella
Isadora Duncan
Isherwood
Ishmael
Ishtar
Isis
Isolde
Isometric

Istanbul
Ithunn
Itinerant
Iussi Bjorling
Ivan
Ivan the Terrible
Ivanhoe
Ivory
Ivy
Iwo Jima
Izmir

Jabba the Hutt
Jabberwocky
Jacintha
Jack Frost
Jackie Robinson
Jackson
Jacob
Jacqueline
Jade
Jake
Jake Barnes
Jalapeno
Jamaica
Jamboree
James
James Bond
Jane
Jane Eyre
Jane Russell
Janet
January
Japonica
Jarvis
Jasmine
Jason
Jasper
Java
Jaworsky
Jazz
Jean
Jeanie Dean
Jeannette
Jeeves
Jefferson
Jell-O
Jellyroll Morton
Jellybean
Jemima

Jenny
Jenny Lind
Jeremy
Jerome
Jerusalem
Jessamine
Jesse
Jesse Jackson
Jessica
Jet
Jeté
Jewel
Jezebel
JFK
Jiffy
Jig
Jill
Jim
Jim Brown
Jimi Hendrix
Jimmie Rodgers
Jingle
Jingo
Jinx
Jitterbug
Joan
Joan Baez
Joan Sutherland
Job
Jocasta
Jocelyn
Jock O'Hazeldean
Joe
Joe Christmas
Joe DiMaggio
Joe Garagiola
Joe Willie Namath
John
John Boy
John Donne
John Paul Jones
John Wellington Wells
John, Paul, George and Ringo
Johnny Appleseed
Johnny Cash
Johnny Weissmuller
Johnson
Jokanaan
Joker
Jolly

Jonah
Jonas Salk
Jonathan
Jonquil
Joralemon
Jordan
Jorge
José
José Carreras
Josephine
Josh
Jove
Joy
J. P. Morgan
J. R.
J. T.
Juanita
Judah
Judah Ben-Hur
Judd
Judy
Julep
Julia
Juliana
Julius
Julius Caesar
Juniper
Junket
Juno
Jupiter
Justin
Justine
Justinian

Kabuki
Kaffir
Kafka
Kahlua
Kalahari
Kalamazoo
Kamakazi
Kamehameha
Kangaroo
Kansas
Karim Abdul-Jabbar
Karl Marx
Karma
Karpov
Kasbah
Kaspar

Katie
Katisha
Kattegat
Katydid
Kawasaki
Kazoo
Keats
Kellogg
Kelly
Kelpie
Kelvin
Kenilworth
Kensington
Kentucky
Kerala
Kerensky
Kerry
Ketchum
Kibitz
Kickapoo
Kicking Bear
Kicking Bird
Kidderminster
Kierkegaard
Kiev
Kildare
Kilimanjaro
Killiecrankie
Kimberley
King Arthur
King Rajaraja
Kinsey
Kinshasa
Kiowa
Kips Bay
Kirby
Kiri Te Kanawa
Kirk Douglas
Kirkpatrick
Kirsten Flagstadt
Kismit
Kissinger
Kitty
Kitty O'Shea
Kiwi
Kliban
Knoxville
Ko-Ko
Kong
Kool and The Gang

Korchnoi
Kosciuszko
Kosher
Krakatoa
Krazy Kat
Kremlin
Kreskin
Krishna
Krishnamurti
Kristofferson
Krum
Kublai Khat
Kumquat
Kurosawa
Kvetch

L.A.
Lacey
Lady Brett
Lady Jane
Lady Macbeth
Lady Sangazure
Ladybells
Ladybird
La Fontaine
Laidlaw
Lallygag
La Lollo
Lamentations
Lana Turner
Launcelot
Lando Calrissian
Landseer
Landslide
Langella
Langston
Langsyne
Lao-tse
Lapwing
Lara
Lardass
Largo
Larissa
Larkins
Larkspur
Lasker
Laverne
Lavinia
Lawrence Tibbets
Lean Bear

Leapyear
Lear
Lefty O'Doul
Legs Diamond
Lehrer
Leia Organa
Leibnitz
Lemon
Lemondrop
Lenin
Lentil
Leo
Leon
Leonardo
Leonie
Leontyne Price
Lepus
Leslie
Lester
Letty Cottin Pogrebin
Levenfish
Lewis
Libby
Liberace
Liberty de Vito
Licketysplit
Light
Lilac
Lilith
Lillian Russell
Lily
Lily Langtry
Lime
Lindsay
Lipton
Litterbug
Little
Little Crow
Little David
Little Egypt
Little Rascal
Little Raven
Little Richard
Little Wolf
Liverpool
Livewire
Livia
Livingston
Liz & Dick
Liza

Liza Doolittle
Lizzie
Lizzie Borden
Llewellyn
Lloyd George
Lobsang Rampa
Lochinvar
Lodovico Sforza
Lohengrin
Lolita
Lollipop
Lombard
Lone Wolf
Lonesome
Lone Star
Long John
Longfellow
Longshot
Looking Glass
Lord and Lady Bellamy
Lord Byron
Lord Kitchener
Lorelei
Lorenzo the Magnificent
Loretta Lynn
Lorna Doone
Lorraine
Lotus
Louis
Louis Seize
Louisa
Love Boat
Lovelace
Lovelady
Lovelorn
Lovey
Löwenbräu
Lucia
Lucifer
Lucille
Lucinda
Lucknow
Lucky
Lucky Lindbergh
Lucky Luciano
Lucrezia Borgia
Lucy Blueberry
Ludwig
Lugalzaggisi
Luigi

107

Luke Skywalker
Lulu
Lupe
Luther
Luther Standing Bear
Lydia
Lyndon
Lynx
Lysander

Mab
Ma Barker
Mabel
MacArthur
MacDiarmid
MacNeil
Macaroni
Macauley
Macavity
Macbeth
Macdonald
Macduff
Machiavelli
Machine Gun Kelly
Machine Gun Lou
Mackintosh
MacNamara
Mad Margaret
Madagascar
Madam Flora
Madame Blavatsky
Madame Butterfly
Madame Curie
Madame Du Barry
Madame Nu
Madcap
Madeira
Madeline
Madison
Madison-Avenue-at-64th Street
Madonna
Madrigal
Mae West
Mag Wheels
Magda
Maggie
Magnet
Magnificat
Magnolia
Magnum

Magpie
Magritte
Mah-jongg
Mahalia
Mahogany
Maidstone
Mainsail
Maisie
Maitland
Major Barbara
Malcolm X
Malory
Malusardi
Mama Rose
Mandingo
Mangas Colorado
Manhattan
Manuelito
Manzanillo
Mao Tse-tung
Maracaibo
Marat and Sade
Marble
Marc Antony
Marcel Proust
Marcello Mastroianni
Marcia
Marco Polo
Margaret
Margaret Rose
Margaret Sanger
Margo
Maria Callas
Maria Montez
Maria Ouspenskaya
Maria Tallchief
Maria Theresa
Marianne Moore
Marie
Marie Antoinette
Marigold
Marilyn Monroe
Marina
Marion
Marion Motley
Mariposa
Marjoram
Marjorie Morningstar
Mark Twain
Marlene

Marleybone
Marlon
Marlowe
Marmaduke Pointdextre
Marmalade
Maroczy
Marrakesh
Mars
Marsala
Marsden
Marshmallow
Martha
Martha Graham
Martin Luther
Martina Orroyó
Mary
Mary McCarthy
Mary Tyler Moore
Mary-ann
Mary-lou
Mary-Margaret
Mary, Queen of Scots
Maryjane
Marzipan
Mascagni
Mason
Massachusetts
Massimo d'Alelio
Masterson
Mata Hari
Matches
Matilda
Matisse
Matt
Matthew
Maude
Maupassant
Maurice
Maverick
Mavis
Max
Maximilian
Maxine
Maxwell
Mayakovska
Maybelline
Mayflower
Mayhem
Mazeltov
Mazzini

McCabe and Mrs. Miller
McCoy
McEnroe
McGuffey
Meadowlark
Meadowlark Lemon
the Meatman
Meddlesome
Medici
Medicine Bottle
Megaera
Mehitabel
Meister Eckhart
Melanie
Melba
Melchior
Melina
Melisande
Melissa
Mellow
Melody
Melungeon
Melville
Memphis
Memsahib
Menassa
Mendelssohn
Mengarini
Mephisto
Mephistopheles
Merce
Mercedes
Mercury
Mercury Morris
Merle Haggard
Merlin
Merrybells
Mersey
Meshach
Mesquite
Messallina
Metchnikoff
Methethany
Methuselah
Metternich
Meyer Lansky
MG
Micawber
Michael
Michelangelo

Mickey Spillane
Mick Jagger
Midas
Midnight
Mies
Mignon
Mikado
Mildred Pierce
Miles
Milhous
Milkweed
Milkwood
Millicent
Milton
Mimi
Mimosa
Mincemeat
Minerva
Minestrone
Minna von Barnhelm
Minnehaha
Minnesota
Minnie
Minnow
Minstrel
Mint
Minx
Mipam
Mirabeau
Miranda
Mirella Freni
Miriam
Miró
Mirth
Mischief
Miss De Mille
Miss Jean Brodie
Miss Pudding
Missie
Mississippi
Missoula
Missouri
Mistress Overdone
Mistress Quickly
Misty Morning
Mittens
Mitzi
Moberly
Mobster
Mocha

Modesty
Modigliani
Modred
Mohammed
Moira Shearer
Moishe Dayan
Mojave
Molasses
Mole
Molière
Moll Flanders
Molly
Moloch
Molotov
Mona
Monday
Moneybags
Monk
Montague
Montana
Monte Christo
Monterey
Montesquieu
Montessori
Montgomery
Montresor
Montserrat Caballe
Monty
Monty Python
Moody
Mookie Wilson
Moonbeam
Moonflower
Moonshine
Moonstone
Moose
Moppet
Mopsa
Morgan Fairchild
Moriarty
Mork and Mindy
Morning Glory
Morocco
Morris
Morrissey
Mortimer
Morton
Moseby
Mosquito
Moth

110

Mothball
Mother Bombie
Mother Cat
Motley
Motorboat
Mott
Mottle
Mountain
Mountjoy
Mouse
Mousemeat
Mousetrap
Moxie
Mozart
Mozzarella
Mr. Christian
Mr. Disraeli
Mr. Gladstone
Mr. Goldstone
Mr. Goodbar
Mr. Rochester
Mr. Sammler
Mr. Stanley
Mrs. Beeton
Mrs. Danvers
Mrs. Miniver
Mrs. Pankhurst
Mrs. Patrick Campbell
Mrs. Robinson
Mrs. Siddons
Mudcat
Muddy Waters
Muezza
Muffin
Muffler
Mugwump
Muhammad Ali
Mularky
Mulberry
Mule
Mull of Kintyre
Mulligan
Mumphy
Munger
Mungojerrie
Murchison
Murdoch
Muriel
Murillo
Murmansk

Murphy
Murray
Murray Hill
Musca
Muscatel
Musetta
Musketeer
Muskrat
Mussorgsky
Mustafa
Mustang
Mustard
Mustardseed
Mutanabi
Myra Breckenridge
Myrtle

Nabisco
Nabob
Nahum
Nameless
Nancy
Nancy Hanks
Nanking
Nankipooh
Nantucket
Naomi
Naples
Napoleon
Napoleon Lajoie
Napoleon Solo
Narcissus
Narragansett
Naseby
Nash
Nashville
Nasser
Natalie
Natasha
Natchez
Nathan
Nathaniel
Nato
Natty
Naughty
Nautilus
Navaho
Navratilova
Naxos
Nebraska

Nebuchadnezzar
Nebula
Ned
Nefertiti
Nehemiah
Nellie
Nellie Melba
Nelson
Nemesis
Nemo
Nepenthe
Neptune
Nero
Nessie
Nestor
Netsuke
Nettles
Network
Nevada
Nevelson
Neville
Nevis
Nevski
Newman
Newport
Newton
Niagara
Nibbles
Nicholas
Nick
Nick Shadow
Nickel
Nicotine
Nielsen
Nietzsche
Nifty
Nigel
Night Flight
Nightcap
Nightingale
Nightowl
Nijinska
Nijinski
Nike
Nimble
Nimitz
Nimrod
Nimzo
Nina
Ninja

Nirvana
No No Nanette
Noah
Noblesse
Noddy
Noel
Noggin
Noguchi
NoHo
Nokomis
Nomad
Nonce
Noose
Nora
Norfolk
Norman
Northcliffe
Northrop
Norton
Norway
Norwood
Nosey
Nostradamus
Notorious
Nottingham
Nova
November
Nowhere
Nugget
Nureyev
Nutmeg

Oakland
Oakley
Oatcake
Obadiah
Oberon
Obi-Wan-Kenobi
Oboe
Obsolete
O'Casey
Occasional
Occupant
Oceans Eleven
Ocelot
Ochre
O'Clock
Octavia
Octavia Hill
October

Octopussy

Oddball

Odell

Odessa

Odin

O'Farrell

Offbeat

Offenbach

Ogden

Ogilvy

Oglethorpe

Ogre

O'Hara

Ohio

O.J.

O.J. Simpson

Okie

Okinawa

Oklahoma

Okra

Olaf

Old Crow

Old Deuteronomy

Old Fitzgerald

Old Ironsides

Oldenburg

Oldtimer

Ole

Olga

Olitski

Olive Oyl

Oliver

Oliver Wendell Holmes

Olympias

Omaha

Omar Khayam

Omar Sharif

Omsk

Ondine

One-Eyed Tony

Oneida

Ontario

Oona

007

Opal

Ophelia

Opium

Opocensky

Oppenheimer

Opportunity

Oral Roberts

Orange

Orangeaid

Orbicular

Orchid

Oregano

Oregon

Orestes

Orff

Oriente

Origami

Orinoco

Orion

Orissa

Orkney

Orlando

Ormuzd

Ornery

Orpheus

Orsino

Ortrud

Orville

Orwell

Osaka

Osawatomie

Oscar

Oscar Wilde

Oshkosh

Osiris

Osman Pasha

Ossian

Oswald

Othello

Otherwise

Otis Redding

Otto

Ottokar

Ouija

Ounce

Our Times

Outback

Outland

Outlaw

Ouzo

Ovaltine

Overalls

Overlong

Overlord

Overmuch

Overtrump

Ovid
Owen Glendower
Oxford
Oxlip
Oyster
Ozone
Ozzie Smith

Pablo
Paddington
Paderewski
Paella
Paganini
Paisley
Paiute
Palmolive
Paloma
Pamela
Pamplona
Panama
Pancake
Pancho Gonzales
Pandemonium
Pandora
Pangurban
Panhandle
Panic
Pannikin
Pansy
Pantaloon
Papa Daddy
Papa Hemingway
Papillon
Papoose
Paprika
Paracelsus
Paraffin
Paris
Parnell
Parpignol
Parsifal
Parsley
Parsnip
Pas de Chat
Pasadena
Pascal
Pascati
Pasha
Passamaquoddy
Pastel

Pasternak
Pastiche
Patagonia
Patches
Patchin
Patchouli
Patchwork
Patience
Patrick
Patton
Paul Revere
Paulo
Pavarotti
Pavlova
Pawnee
Pawtucket
Peabody
Peaches
Peanut
Peapod
Pearl
Peaseblossom
Peasoup
Pecksniff
Pedro
Peebles
Peep-Bo
Peewee
Pegasus
Pekoe
Pelleas
Pendergast
Pendragon
Penelope
Pennyroyal
Pennyworth
Penzance
Peony
Pepper
Pepper Martin
Pepperidge
Peppermint
Pepsi
Pequod
Percival
Percy Bysshe Shelley
Perdita
Periwinkle
Perkins
Persephone

Perseus
Persimmon
Personality
Pete Seeger
Peter
Peter Porter
Peter the Great
Peter, Paul and Mary
Petipa
Petitpoint
Peto
Petrarch
Petrosian
Petrov
Petrovich
Petruchio
Pettigrew
Petunia
Phaedra
Phantom
Pharaoh
Philidor
Philip
Philip the Fair
Philip the Handsome
Philomena
Philpot
Phineas T. Barnum
Phoebe
Phoenix
Phyllis
Pianissimo
Picasso
Piccolo
Pickerel
Pickles
Pickwick
Piecrust
Pierre
Pietro Forquet
Pigpen
Pillsbury
Pimlico
Pimpernel
Pina Bausch
Pinafore
Pinch
Pineapple
Ping-Pong
Pinkerton

Pinocchio
Pinochle
Pin Stripe
Pinup
Pinwheel
Pip
Pippa
Pirandello
Pirate
Pirc
Pirozhki
Pisces
Pish-Tish
Pissarro
Pistachio
Pistol
Piston
Pitcairn
Pitstop
Pittsburgh
Pitti-Sing
Pizza
Pizzicato
Placido Domingo
Plantagenet
Plato
Plimsoll
Pliny
Plum
Pluto
Pocahontas
Poco
Podsnap
Poincaré
Poindexter
Poins
Poitier
Pokeweed
Pola Negri
Poldark
Pollock
Pollux
Polly Flinders
Polonius
Polynesia
Pomander
Pomegranate
Pompey
Pondicherry
Ponziani

Pooh-Bah
Popcorn
Popeye
Popov
Poppy
Porgy
Porkpie
Porsche
Porter
Portia
Portland
Portnoy
Poseidon
Postlethwaite
Potrero
Potter
Poughkeepsie
Pounce
Powderpuff
Powhatan
Preacher
Prentiss
Presley
Preston
Pretoria
Pretty Boy Floyd
Pretzel
Primadonna
Prime Ribs
Primrose
Prince Andrew
Prince Gruffydd of Gwynedd
Prince McJunkins III
Prince Potëmkin
Princeton
Private Willis
Prometheus
Promiscuous
Propitious
Prospero
Proust
Prudence
Ptolemy
Puccini
Puck
Pudding
Pukka
Pulitzer
Puma
Pumblechook

Pumpernickel
Pumpkin
Purcell
Pushet
Pushkin
Pushpin
Pussy Galore
Pussytoes
Pussywillow
Puzzle
Pygmalion
Pythagoras
Pytor
Pywacket

Quadrille
Quaint
Quaker
Quality
Quantrill
Quantum
Quark
Quarrelsome
Quarterdeck
Quartermaster
Quarto
Quasimodo
Quatrocento
Queen Anne
Queen Christina
Queen Elizabeth
Queen Mary
Queen Mother
Queensberry
Queerstreet
Quenton
Querulous
Questionable
Quetzalcoatl
Quibble
Quiche
Quicksilver
Quicktime
Quiddity
Quidnunc
Quill
Quimby
Quince
Quincy
Quinine

Quint
Quintana Roo
Quirky
Quiver
Quivive
Quixote
Quizzical
Qum
Quodlibet
Quonset
Quorum
Quota
Quotidian

Rabbit
Rabelais
Rabindranath Tagore
Rabinowitz
Raccoon
Rachmaninoff
Racine
Rackety
Radames
Radar
Radcliffe
Radiant
Raeburn
Railroad
Raimondo
Rainbow
Raindrop
Raintree
Rajah
Ralph Rackstraw
Ralph Waldo Emerson
Ramakrishna
Rambler
Rameses
Ramona
Ramphis
Randall Jarrell
Randolph
Random
Rangoon
Ransom
Raoul
Rap Brown
Raphael
Raponi Longo
Rapparee

Rappoport
Rapscallion
Rapture
Rapunzel
Raquel Welch
Rarebit
Rascal
Raskolnikov
Rasmussen
Raspberry
Rasputin
Ratatattat
Ratner
Ratrap
Ratsbane
Rauschenberg
Ravel
Raven
Ravioli
Rawalpindi
Ray Charles
Ready
Reality
Reaper
Rearaxle
Rebecca
Rebel
Recalcitrant
Reckless
Recumbent
Red
Red Cloud
Red Conkright
Red Jacket
Red Schoendienst
Red Sleeves
Red Sovine
Redbird
Redbud
Redeye
Redford
Redneck
Reefer
Refrigerator
Regan
Reggie
Reggie Jackson
Reginald Bunthorne
Régine
Relish

117

Reluctant
Remarkable
Rembrandt
Remington
Remus
Renata
Renault
Renfrew
Reno
Renoir
Reo Speedwagon
Reprisal
Respighi
Resurrection
Reti
Retsina
Reuben
Rhapsody
Rhett Butler
Rhoda
Rhubarb
Rhum-Rhum
Rialto
Richard
Richard Burbage
Richard the Lionheart
Richelieu
Rickenbacker
Ridley
Riesling
Riff
the Rifleman
Rigmarole
Rigoletto
Riley
Rilke
Rilla
Rimbaud
Ringo
Rinso
Rio
Ripley
Rita Hayworth
Riviera
Rizzoli
Rob Roy
Robert E. Lee
Robert Merrill
Robert the Bruce
Robert the Devil

Roberta Peters
Roberto
Robespierre
Robin
Robin Goodfellow
Robin Hood
Robin Oakapple
Robinson
Rochester
Rock Hudson
Rockefeller
Rockford
Rocky I
Rocky II
Rocky III
Rodgers and Hammerstein
Rodolfo
Roger
Roland Hooks
Rollercoaster
Rollie Fingers
Rolls
Romanov
Romeo & Juliet
Rommel
Romney
Romulus
Rondo
Ronsard
Ronzoni
Rookie
Roosevelt
Rosa Luxemburg
Rosa Ponsell
Rosabelle Furcap
Rosalie
Rosalind
Rose
Rose Maybud
Roseanne Roseannadanna
Rose Hill
Rosemary
Rosenkrantz
Rosewall
Rosie Casals
Rosina
Rossini
Rossolimo
Rothesay
Rothko

Rothschild
Rotterdam
Rough
Roughhouse
Rousseau
Roxie
R2D2
Rubens
Ruby
Ruby Keeler
Rudolf
Rudyard Kipling
Rue
Ruffles
Rugby
Ruggero Raimondo
Rumania
Rumpelstiltskin
Runnymede
Rupert
Rushmore
Ruskin
Russell
Rutabaga
Ruth
Rutherford
Rutledge
Ruy Lopez
Rye

Sable
Sabotage
Sabrina
Sacco
Sacharissa
Sacheverel
Sackcloth
Sackville
Sacramento
Safflower
Saffron
Sagan
Sage
Sagebrush
Saginaw
Sagittarius
Sahara
Sahib
Sailboat
Saint Tropez

Saki
Saladin
Salamander
Salami
Salisbury
Salmagundi
Salome
Salonika
Salsify
Sam
Sam Colt
Sam Pepys
Samantha
Samarkand
Samba
Samson
Samuel Gompers
Samurai
Sancho the Great
Sandbag
Sandburg
Sandhog
Sandusky
Sanford
Sang Chong
Sangaree
Sang-froid
Santa Anna
Santayana
Sapodilla
Sappho
Sara Teasdale
Sarah
Sarah Bernhardt
Saratoga
Sardine
Sardinia
Sargasso
Sargent
Sargon
Sarsaparilla
Sartoris
Sashimi
Sassafras
Sassenach
Sassetta
Sassoon
Saturday Night Live
Saturn
Savannah

Savonarola
Sawbones
Sawdust
Scallywag
Scampi
Scaramouche
Scarlatti
Scarlett O'Hara
Scarpia
Scheherazade
Schnitzel
Schopenhauer
Schubert
Scirocco
Scorpius
Scott
Screwtape
Scrimshaw
Scully
Scupper
Sean Connery
Sebastian
Seelbach
Sejanus
Selima
Selkirk
Serena
Serpico
Sesame
Setebos
Seth
Sevareid
Seymour Glass
Shackleford
Shadow
Shafer Suggs
Shakespeare
Shallow
Shampoo
Shane
Shanghai
Shangri-la
Sharpless
Shaunessy
Sheba
Shenandoah
Sherbet
Sherlock Holmes
Shirley
Shoestring

Shōgun
Sholom Aleichem
Shoofly
Shortcake
Shortstop
Shoshone
Shostakovich
Shotgun
Shreveport
Shufala Kid
Shutterbug
Shuttlecock
Sibelius
Siberia
Sidelong
Sideswipe
Sideways
Sidewinder
Sidney Greenstreet
Siegfried
Siegfried Sassoon
Sienna
Sigmund Freud
Signora
Silence
Silky
Silly Putty
Silver
Silver Belle
Simon
Simon and Garfunkel
Simple
Simplicity
Simpson
Sinatra
Sing-Song
Singapore
Sioux
'Sippi
Sir Balan
Sir Balin
Sir Bedivere
Sir Daspard Murgatroyd
Sir Galahad
Sir Gawain
Sir Geraint
Sir Launcelot
Sir Pelleas
Sir Perceval
Sir Tristram

Sirius
Sitting Bull
Skeezix
Skipper
Skippy
Skokie
Slapstick
Slate
Sleeper
Sloopy
Sly Stone
Small
Smallfry
Smidgeon
Smoke
Smoky
Smudge
Snafu
Snail's Pace
Snake
Snapdragon
Snoof
Snooker
Snoopy
Snooze
Snopes
Snorkel
Snorri Sturluson
Snowball
Snowdrop
Snowfire
Snowflake
Snowflower
Snowhite
Snowman
Snowpea
Snowy
Snug
So What
Soapbox
Soap Suds
Socks
Socrates
Sodawater
Softball
Softshoe
Softsoap
Software
SoHo
Solange

Solfa
Solicitude
Solidarity
Solitude
Solomon
Solon
Solway
Sombrero
Someday
Sominex
Sonar
Sonata
Sonnet
Sonny and Cher
Sonya
Sooty
Sophia
Sophie
Sophocles
Soporific
Sorcerer
Sorehead
Sorrel
Sorrento
Soufflé
Soul Brother
Soup du Jour
Sourdough
South Pacific
Southwark
Sovereign
Spackle
Spam
Sparafucile
Sparkle Plenty
Sparkplug
Sparks
Sparky Lyle
Spartacus
Spassky
Spatter
Speakeasy
Speedball
Speedway
Spellbound
Spencer
Spendthrift
Spider
Spinach
Spindleshanks

Spindrift
Spinoza
Splash
Splashdown
Spock
Spokane
Spokes
Spoletta
Sporran
Sporting Life
Spotted Tail
Spumone
Spurious
Squadcar
Squaredance
Squarepeg
Squareroot
Squash Blossom
Squashbug
Squeak
Squeeze
Squirrel
St. Louie Louie
Stagestruck
Stalemate
Stallone
Stanford
Stanislavsky
Stanley
Stanyan
Star
Stardust
Starsky and Hutch
Startrek
Starveling
Staten Island
Steamboat
Steamheat
Steelhead
Steeplechase
Steeplejack
Steerage
Stella
Stella Dallas
Stella Rondo
Stendhal
Stephanie
Stephano
Sterling
Stethoscope

Stetson
Stevedore
Stewart
Stiletto
Stingo
Stokely
Stonehenge
Stopgap
Stormalong
Stradivarius
Stranger
Stratford
Strathspey
Stravinsky
Strawberry
Strawberry Shortcake
the Streak
Streep
Streetcar
Stripes
Stripey
Stromboli
Stubbs
Studs Lonigan
Stuyvesant
Styx
Subaru
Sublet
Succotash
Sue Ellen
Sugar Baby
Sugarbug
Sugarplum
Sukiyaki
Sullivan
Sum Total
Summa Cum Laude
Summer
Sun Yat-sen
Sunburst
Sundance
Sunday
Sunflower
Sunshine
Sunsweet
Superfriend
Surabaya
Surrey
Sushi
Susie

Susquehanna
Sutton
Suzie Wong
Suzuki
Svengali
Swami
Swanson
Swansong
S.W.A.T.
Swedenborg
Sweeney Todd
Sweepstakes
Sweet Evening Breeze
Sweet Molly Malone
Sweetheart
Sweetmeat
Sweetpants
Sweetsop
Sybil
Sybil Thorndyke
Sycorax
Sydney
Syllabub
Sylvana Mangano
Sylvester
Sylvia
Sylvia Plath
Sylvia Townsend Warner
Synge
Syzygy
Szabo
Szechuan

Tabasco
Tabitha
Tacitus
Tad
Tadpole
Taffy
Tag
Taglioni
Tahiti
Tailpipe
Tailspin
Taj Mahal
Tal
Talbot Mundy
Taliesin
Tallahassee
Tallahatchie

Talleyrand
Tallulah
Tally Ho
Tallyrand
Tam O'Shanter
Tamale
Tamara, Queen of Georgia
Tamarind
Tambourine
Tammanay
Tammy Wynette
Tamora
Tampa
Tangerine
Tangier
Tango
Tank Car
Tannhäuser
Tant Pis
Tanya
Tapdance
Tapioca
Tara
Tarantella
Tarantula
Tarbaby
Target
Tarot
Tarragon
Tartuffe
Tarzan and Jane
Tashkent
Tasmania
Tassle
Tasso
Tatiana
Tattletale
Taurus
Tavistock
Taxi
Tchaikovsky
Teacup
Teakettle
Teamster
Teapot
Tecumseh
Teddy
Teen Angel
Teenybopper
Telly

Temperance
Temple Drake
Templeton
Ten Broeck
Tenerife
Tennessee
Tenspot
Tentsel
Tepee
Terpsichore
Terrence
Testtube
Teufel
Tewkesbury
Texas
Thackeray
Thanatopsis
Thane
Thankless
Thataway
Theodora
Thermos
Thimble
Thistledown
Thomas Aquinas
Thomasina
Thor
Thoreau
Thornton
Thucydides
Thumper
Thundarr
Thunder
Thunderball
Thursday
Thyme
Tiberius
Tiburon
Tic-Tac-Toe
Tidal Wave
Tiddlywink
Tiffany
Tiger
Tiger Lily
Tigger
Tigris
Timberline
Timbuctoo
Timothy Higgins
Tin Whistle

Tina
Tinhorn
Tinker
Tinkerbell
Tintoretto
Tintype
Tip-Top
Tippoo Sahib
Tippecanoe
Tipple
Tiresias
Tisiphone
Titania
Titian
Titicaca
Titus
Toast
Tobacco Red
Tobermory
Toby
Toby Belch
Todd
Toff
Tolitha
Tollgate
Tolstoy
Tom
Tom Jefferson
Tom Jones
Tom Rakewell
Tom-Tom
Tom Tucker
Tom Tunnicliffe
Tomahawk
Tombstone
Tommy Tune
Tonsils
Tootsie
Top Job
Topaz
Topeka
Topheavy
Topsider
Torpid
Torquemada
Tortoni
Tosca
Tosspot
Totem Pole
Tottenham

Touchstone
Toulouse-Lautrec
Toupé Jay
Tourmaline
Tousle
Tout
Tracy
Trade In
Trafalgar
Trailblazer
Transamerica
Transylvania
Trapper John
Travis
Travolta
Treacle
Treat
Trelawny
Tribeca
Triborough
Tribulation
Tribune
Trifle
Trilby
Trilobite
Trinculo
Tristan
Tristesse
Triumph
Trojan
Trombone
Trompovsky
Trotsky
Trouble
True West
Truelove
Truffles
Trumpet
Tsarina
T. S. Eliot
T-Square
Tu-tu
Tubular
Tucson
Tuesday
Tug o' War
Tugboat
Tulip
Tulsa
Tumbleweed

Tuna
Tunnel Vision
Tuppence
Turk
Turner
Turnip
Turpentine
Turpin
Turquoise
Turtle Bay
Tuscarora
Tutankhamen
Tutti-Frutti
Tuxedo
Tweedledee
Tweedledum
Tweezer
Twickenham
Twiggy
Twilight
Twining
Twinkle
Twist
Twyla
Ty Cobb
Tyrannosaurus
Tyrone
Tz'u Hsi

Ubiquitous
U-Boat
Uccello
Udall
Uganda
Ugolini
Ukulele
Ultrabrite
Ulysses
Umber
Umberto
Umbra
Umbrage
Umbrella
Umlaut
Umpire
Unabashed
Unbeatable
Unbeknownst
Uncanny
Uncas

Uncie
Uncle Floyd
Uncle Gustav
Uncle Sam
Underfoot
Undertow
Underworld
Unearthly
Unemployed
Unfruitful
Ungainly
Ungrateful
Union Jack
Unravelled
Unruffled
Untermeyer
Upbeat
Uppercrust
Uppitty
Upsidedown
Upstairs and Downstairs
Uptown
Uranus
Urchin
Urdu
Uriah
Ursa Major
Ursa Minor
Ursula
Urubamba
Usher
Utah
Utamaro
Utopia
Utrillo
U-Turn
Uwe Blab

Vagabond
Valda Setterfield
Valencia
Valentine
Valentino
Valenzuela
Valéry
Valhalla
Valiant
Vallejo
Van Dyke
Van Gogh

Van Ness
Vancouver
Vandal
Vanderbilt
Vandewater
Vanessa
Vanilla
Vanity Fair
Vanzetti
Variety
Varsity
Varuna
Vaughan
Vega
Vegas
Vegetable Beef
Velásquez
Velvet
Venezuela
Vengeance
Venice
Venus
Veracity
Verbena
Vercingetorix
Verdigris
Verlaine
Vermeer
Vermont
Veronese
Veronica Lake
Verrazano
Verrocchio
Vertigo
Vespasian
Vespers
Vesta
Vestpocket
Vesuvius
Vibes
Vicar
Victor
Victoria
Victoria and Albert
Vida Blue
Video
Vienna
Vigée Lebrun
Viking
Villa Lobos

Vinaigrette
Vincent
Viola
Viola Osgood Dunne
Violet
Violetta
Virgil
Virgin
Virginia Woolf
Virgo
Viscount
Visigoth
Viva
Vivaldi
Vivekananda
V. J.
Vladimir
Vladivostok
Volcano
Volkswagen
Voltaire
Volvo
Von Clausewitz
Voodoo
Vorpal
Voyager
V. P.
Vulcan

Waco
Waddles
Waffle
Wafik el Sanadi
Wagner
Wags
Wahoo
Waif
Wakefield
Waldorf
Walla Walla
Wallace
Wallah
Walleye
Wallflower
Wallstreet
Walnut
Walpole
Walrus
Walsingham
Walter Avarelli

Wampum
Wanda
Wanton
Warburton
Wardance
Warfarin
Warhol
Warlock
Warlord
Warpaint
Warren
Warwick
Washboard Sam
Washday
Washington
Wassermann
Watchcap
Waterbury
Watercress
Watergate
Waterloo
Watermelon
Waterspout
Watson
Waverly
Wayfarer
Waylon Jennings
Weatherman
Webster
Wedgwood
Wednesday
Weenie Beenie
Weepy
Welfare
Wellfleet
Wellington
Wells Fargo
Wembley
Wenceslas
Wentworth
Werewolf
Werner
Wesley
Westminster
Wharton
Wheatgerm
Wheedle
Whereabouts
Whiplash
Whippoorwill

Whirlaway
Whirligig
Whirlwind
Whisky
Whisper
Whistler
Whistlestop
White Cloud
Whiteberry
Whitewall
Whitewash
Whitey Kurowski
Whitie
Whitman
Whittington
Whizzbang
Wichita
Wicked Wilson Picket
Wicket
Wigginton
Wigglesworth
Wigwam
Wilander
Wilberforce
Wilbur
Wildfire
Wilhelm
Wilhelmina
Willa
William
William the Conqueror
William Wallace
Willibald
Willie Loman
Willie Mays
Willie McGee
Willie Mosconi
Willie Nelson
Willie Wiggins
Willoughby
Willow
Wilson
Wimbledon
Wimple
Wimpy Lassiter
Winchester
Windflower
Windjammer
Windmill
Windowsill

Windshield
Windsor
Winfield
Wink
Winkle
Winston
Winterset
Winthrop
Wireless
Wiseacre
Wishbone
Wisp
Wistful
Wittgenstein
Wizard
Wobbly
Wockenfuss
Wodka
Woebegone
Woeful
Wolfsbane
Woodpecker
Woodstock
Woodward
Woody
Wookie
Woolworth
World B. Free
World War II
Wormwood
Wotan
Wowkle
Wrangler
Wraparound
Wriggly
Wunderbar
Wyatt Earp
Wyoming

Xanadu
Xanthippe
Xanthopoulou
Xanthus
Xavier
Xaviera
Xelowski
Xenia
Xenobia
Xenophon
Xerox

Xerxes
Xian
Xiang
Xicara
Ximinez
Xingu
Xio
Xiomi
Xiong
Xioni
Xiques
Xochimilcho
Xochitl
X-Ray
Xu
Xuthus
Xwack
Xylophone

Yablonovvy
Yakima
Yale
Yalta
Yam
Yamadori
Yamaha
Yamasaki
Yang Tze
Yankee Doodle
Yarborough
Yardarm
Yarmouth
Yarmulke
Yarrow
Yashmak
Y. A. Tittle
Yazoo
Yearsley
Yeats
Yehudi Menuhin
Yellow Eyes
Yellowstone
Yenta
Yeoman
Yesterday
Yevtushenko
Yggdrasil
Yiewsley
Yinchwan
Ying and Yang

Yippee
Yoda
Yofi
Yogi
Yogurt
Yoiks
Yoko Ono
Yokohama
Yolo
Yom Kippur
Yonkers
Yorkshire
Yoruba
Yosemite
You Damn Fool Cat
Youngblood
Yucatán
Yucca
Yukon
Yuletide
Yum Yum

Zabaglione
Zachary
Zaftig
Zambesi
Zany
Zanzibar
Zapata
Zara
Zaragosa
Zarathustra
Zarzuela
Zebedee
Zebra
Zebulon
Zebunissa
Zeke
Zelda
Zelig
Zen
Zenana
Zenda
Zenger
Zenith
Zeno
Zephaniah
Zephyr
Zeppelin
Zermatt

Zernike
Zero
Zeta
Zethus
Zeus
Ziegfeld
Zilpah
Zimbabwe
Zingaro
Zinnia
Zinzendorf
Zip and Zap
Zipangu
Zippora
Zircon
Zither
Ziti
Zloty
Zodiac

Zoë
Zoetrope
Zola
Zomba
Zooey
Zoom
Zoro
Zorrilla
Zoser
Zounds
Zox
Zsa Zsa
Zsigmondy
Zsu Zsa
Zucana
Zucchetto
Zucchini
Zuleika Dobson